Theodore Hoe Mead

Horsemanship for Women

Theodore Hoe Mead

Horsemanship for Women

ISBN/EAN: 9783744662864

Printed in Europe, USA, Canada, Australia, Japan

Cover: Foto ©Thomas Meinert / pixelio.de

More available books at **www.hansebooks.com**

HORSEMANSHIP FOR WOMEN

BY

THEODORE H. MEAD

WITH ILLUSTRATIONS BY GRAY PARKER

NEW YORK
HARPER & BROTHERS, FRANKLIN SQUARE
1887

CONTENTS.

PART I.

AMATEUR HORSE-TRAINING 1

LESSON
I. COMING TO THE WHIP 15
II. TO HOLD THE BIT LIGHTLY (*Flexion de la mâchoire*), USING THE CURB 21
III. TO HOLD THE BIT LIGHTLY, USING THE SNAFFLE . . 24
IV. TO LOWER THE HEAD 25
V. TO BEND THE NECK TO RIGHT AND LEFT, WITH THE REINS HELD BELOW THE BIT (*Flexions de l'encolure*) 32
VI. TO BEND THE NECK TO RIGHT AND LEFT, WITH THE REINS THROWN OVER THE NECK 35
VII. TO MOVE THE CROUP TO RIGHT AND LEFT WITH THE WHIP 38
VIII. MOUNTED 41
IX. MOUNTED (*continued*) 48
X. THE WALK 51
XI. TO MOVE THE CROUP WITH HEEL AND WHIP (*Pirouette renversée*) 52
XII. TO GUIDE "BRIDLEWISE" 55
XIII. THE TROT 58
XIV. THE GALLOP, HAND-GALLOP, AND CANTER 64
XV. THE PIROUETTE, DEUX PISTES, PASSAGE 71
XVI. BACKING 75
XVII. RIDING IN CIRCLES.—CHANGE OF LEADING FOOT . . 79

PART II.

	PAGE
ETIQUETTE IN THE SADDLE	87
Dress	88
The Mount	91
Mounting	92
The Start	99
On which Side to Ride	100
The Seat	102
On the Road	107
The Pace	112
Turning	112
The Groom	116

PART III.

LEAPING	118

PART IV.

BUYING A SADDLE-HORSE	132
Parts and "Points" of the Horse, Alphabetically Arranged	135
List of Diseases and Defects	148
INDEX	157

ILLUSTRATIONS.

	PAGE
Coming to the Whip	6
A good Saddle	13
A properly fitted Curb-chain	16
Flexion of the Jaw—using the Curb	22
Lowering the Head	26
Punishment in case of Resistance	27
"Pulling the Hands steadily Apart"	33
To Bend the Neck to Right or Left, with the Reins below the Bits	34
Getting the Horse "Light in Hand"	35
Pulling on the Right Rein	36
Moving the Croup one step to the Right	39
Getting a Horse accustomed to Skirts	42
Showing Reins in Left Hand	43
Advancing at touch of Heel	44
Stopping at touch of Whip on Back	45
The Walk (Colt in Training)	46
Bending the Neck to Right and Left	49
Moving the Croup with the Heel and Whip	53
Guiding Bridlewise (Turning to the Right)	56
The Canter	65
Ordinary Pirouette	71
Going on "Deux Pistes"	72
The Passage	73
Backing	76
Reins in Hand	77

ILLUSTRATIONS.

	PAGE
Act of changing Reins	77
Leading with the Right Fore-foot	80
Leading with the Left Fore-foot	82
Ready to Mount	94
"One, Two, Three"	95
Placing the Foot in the Stirrup	96
Position in Saddle	97
A Square and Proper Seat	103
Method of holding the Reins in both Hands	111
Approaching a Fence	119
A Water Jump	121
Rising to the Leap	127
Coming Down	129
Parts and "Points"	136
The sort of Horse to Buy	146
The sort of Horse not to Buy	149

HORSEMANSHIP FOR WOMEN.

PART I.
AMATEUR HORSE-TRAINING.

"My *dear*," said my wife, "you don't mean to say you have *bought that* horse?"

"Why, yes, indeed," replied I; "and very cheap, too. And why not?"

"You will never get your money back," said she, "no matter how cheap you have bought him. Don't keep him. Send him back before it is too late."

It was a sultry July morning, and my wife stood on the farm-house porch, in provokingly fresh attire, while I held my new acquisition by the bridle in the scorching sun; and just recovering as I was from illness, this conversation struck me as really anything but *tonic* in its character. However, bracing myself up, I replied, "But I don't want to get my money back; I intend to train him for my own use under the saddle."

"Oh, you can never do anything with that great

horse. Why, he is the awkwardest brute I ever saw. Just look at him now!"

In fact, his appearance was anything but beautiful at that moment. His Roman nose, carried a long way forward and a little on one side, gave him somewhat the air of a camel; his coat showed no recent acquaintance with the brush; and as he stood there sleepily in the sun, with one hind-leg hitched up, he did not present at all a picture to charm a lady's eye. Nevertheless, he was, in fact, a reasonably well-made horse, a full black, fifteen and three-quarter hands high, sound, kind, and seven years old.

"He's just horrid," said my wife.

"Oh, that's nothing," said I; "that's only a bad habit he has. We will soon cure him of such slovenly tricks. Just see what good points he has. His legs are a little long, to be sure, but they are broad, and have excellent hoofs; his breast is narrow, but then it is deep; and that large nostril was not given him for nothing. You will see he will run like a race-horse."

"If you once get him started you can never stop him," said my wife. "You know how he pulls, and how nervous he is. He will go till he drops. You are not strong enough to ride such a horse."

"Oh, nonsense," said I; "you can see that there is no mischief in him. Look what a kind eye he has! The fact is, horses are often very sensitive; and while this one may never have been cruelly treated, yet he has been misunderstood, and his feelings hurt a great many times a day. Human beings are the only things he seems afraid of. As for his awkward carriage, it is no worse than that of the farm hand who has made such a failure of trying to use him, and who is, nevertheless, when he stands up straight, a well-made, good-looking fellow. A little careful handling will make that animal as different from his present self as a dandified English sergeant is from the raw recruit he once was. What do you think of his name? It is Sambo."

But my wife was not to be led off on any side question, and after intimating that such a plebeian appellation struck her as quite suitable, she continued: "Now you know that Mr. ——" (the farmer of whom I purchased) "knows a great deal more about horses than you do; you must admit that, for he has been buying and selling and driving them all his life, and *he* doesn't like him, or he wouldn't sell so cheap; and as for training him, for my part I don't believe horse-training can be learned out of books, as a woman would learn a receipt for making cake. Do get him to take the horse back!"

Now I have a great respect for my wife's opinion in general, and in this particular case all her points seemed well taken.

The horse was tall, and I was short; he was excitable, and I hadn't the strength of a boy; he was very awkward, and I had never trained a horse in my life.

However, I had been reading up a little on the subject, and feeling the confidence in myself which a very little knowledge is apt to impart, I was determined to try my hand.

I had remarked that there was a certain French system which was, in the several works I had consulted, always spoken of with respect as a complete and original method, so I obtained a copy of the book, in which is set forth the *Méthode d'Équitation basée sur de nouveaux Principes, par F. Baucher*, and having disentangled (no easy task) what was really practical from the enveloping mass of conceited sham scientific nonsense, I had numbered the margin so as to make a series of simple progressive lessons of half an hour each. The volume in question, which was not, by-the-bye, the present improved edition, I now produced in a somewhat dog-eared condition from under my arm. My wife, seeing that remonstrance was of no avail, took a seat on the veranda, so as to be ready to advise and assist, while my excellent friends, the farmer and his wife, came out "to see the circus," as they said, and established themselves in suitable midsummer attitudes, with countenances of amused expectation.

"The first few lessons must be given on foot," said I, and spreading my Baucher open upon the "horse-block," I proceeded to carry out its first injunction by placing myself, with riding-whip under my arm, in front of the horse, which was already saddled and bridled, and "looking him kindly in the face." He bore my gaze with equanimity, but when the riding-whip was produced he started violently; and when I raised my hand to pat his neck reassuringly he threw up his head and ran back. This evidently was not temper, but alarm. Clearly, moral suasion was not the kind that had been used with him hitherto. In plain English, he had been beaten on the head; and it was some time before he got over the impression made by such ill-treatment and ceased dodging at every sudden motion on my part.

However, a lump of sugar gave the poor fellow more confidence, and, avoiding all brusque movements, I went on to give him the first lesson of the Baucher series, viz., *To Come to the Whip*.

It is encouraging for beginners that this lesson, while producing conspicuous results, is in most cases very easy. In less than half an hour my audience was not a little surprised to see Sambo come to me at the slightest motion of the whip, and follow me about with neck arched, ears pricked up, and eyes lustrous with the unwonted pleasure of comprehending and voluntarily carrying out his master's wishes.

"Well, that's very pretty," said the farmer; "but what's the good of it?"

This criticism, it may be remarked, he continued to repeat at every step in the horse's education. He did not "see the good" of a double bridle with two bits.

He did not see the good of teaching the horse to relax the muscles of his jaw and to hold the bit lightly in the mouth. He did not see the good of suppling the various muscles of the neck, on which, nevertheless, depend to a surprising degree the balance of the whole body and the easy motion of the limbs. In fact, he main-

COMING TO THE WHIP.

tained his attitude of amused and good-natured incredulity until one day, after about three weeks, I rode Sambo into the lawn, his neck arched and tail displayed, and, with the reins hanging on my little finger, made him cut circles and figure eights of all sizes at a spanking trot.

Then my good farmer gave up, and said he really

would hardly have believed it could be the same horse. What is more, he took off his own driving horses "the overdrawn check-reins" by which he had been hauling their noses up into as near a horizontal line as possible, and allowed them to carry their heads in a more natural manner.

The afternoon of his first lesson Sambo was put in double harness for a drive of ten or twelve miles, during which he annoyed me excessively by his restless dancing and fretting, so that next morning I expected to have to begin all over again; but, to my satisfaction, he had forgotten nothing, and came towards me at the first motion of the whip, so that I passed on to the *Flexions de la Mâchoire*, which we translate as the *suppling of the muscles of the jaw*. Here I came upon my first difficulty, and it lasted me several days. It was, however, the only serious one in my whole course, and from subsequent experience I am satisfied that my own awkwardness and disposition to compel obedience by main force were the principal causes of it.

However, success soon rewarded my perseverance, and I had the satisfaction of feeling the iron grip of the bit relax, and seeing the nose brought in and the face assume a perpendicular position.

Without at present going further into detail, I will simply say that at the expiration of a month, during which Sambo had been driven double almost daily, his education for the saddle had so far advanced that his head was admirably carried, his trot was greatly improved—his walk always had been light and swift—he could trot sideways to the right or left, could pirouette to the right or to the left on the hind-feet or on the fore-feet, responding to the pressure of the rein upon his neck or of the leg against his side, while he had become so steady that I could fire at a mark with a pistol from his back.

All this was very satisfactory progress, especially in view of my total inexperience, poor health, and the heat of the weather; but there is no doubt that any active young girl of sixteen or eighteen can do the like, for it was accomplished not by any mysterious or difficult process, nor by any exertion of physical strength, but by patiently following out, step by step, the processes which I am about to describe, and which are substantially those of Baucher, adapted to the use of a person of total inexperience, and that person a lady.

If any such, having accompanied me thus far, feels the impulse to try to improve her own mount, I will confide to her the fact that the incidents narrated really occurred within the last few years not a hundred miles from New York; and I hope that the following propositions, which are literally true, will help to encourage her to an undertaking in which she will find amusement, exercise, and a discipline as useful to herself as to her horse:

1. If, as is very likely, you feel a little afraid of your

horse, you may be assured that your horse is a great deal more afraid of you.

2. If you can only make clear to him what you wish him to do, he will try his best to do it, and will feel amply repaid for his efforts by a few kind words and caresses.

3. His narrow brain can entertain only one idea at once, and therefore only one problem, and that a simple one, must be given him at a time.

4. Once the problem is mastered, a very little practice makes the performance of the task instinctive, so that it will be performed at the proper signal, even against his own will, provided his mind is occupied with something else.

This course of lessons is prepared with these facts in view.

"But is horse-breaking a fitting amusement for young ladies?" a mother asks, and with an air indicating that to her, at least, a reply seems quite unnecessary. My dear madam, it is not horse-breaking we are talking of, but horse-training, which is a very different thing. There are, doubtless, many women who could break a colt if they chose, but it is an undertaking which we certainly do not recommend. In the "breaking to harness" of an untamed horse there is naturally included more or less of training, but the essential lesson to be taught is that it is useless to resist the will of man, for sooner or later the horse will test the question, and put forth every effort to throw off control. When, however, panting and exhausted, he finally submits, he has learned the necessary lesson; and whether it be after a long fight with a brutal rough-rider, or a physically painless struggle with an adroit Rarey, he has learned it for life. Henceforth he accepts the supremacy of the human race, and, unless under the goad of maddening pain or terror, will never, save in rare instances, really rebel; obeying not men only, but women, children, and even the very tools and implements of man, so that a dog may lead him by the bridle. Like a spoiled child, however, a horse will sometimes presume upon indulgence, and, to use a mother's phrase, will try to see how far he can go.

At such times he is best opposed not by violence, but by firmness, reinforced, perhaps, now and then by a sharp cut with the whip, which, given unexpectedly at the precise moment of disobedience, will have the settling effect ascribed to the time-honored nursery "spank," and will bring him to his senses. Generally, however, what seems insubordination is in reality nervousness, which requires soothing, not punishment, and which you will be careful not to increase by fidgeting or by brusque movements of the reins. Even when severity is needed, a reproof in a cold, stern tone is often more effective than the lash.

Thousands of young girls, who for various reasons cannot ride in winter, have every summer within reach horses quite as good as the average of those at city riding-schools, but which they are never allowed to mount.

They look wistfully at the honest animals, longing for the exercise which would be so beneficial to their health and to their physical development, while so delightfully exhilarating to their spirits; but one horse is pronounced "skittish," another "hard-mouthed," and so on to the end. Nevertheless, some enterprising damsel manages to overcome all opposition, and, skirted, hatted, gloved, sets off in fine spirits. The horse, accustomed to the resistance of a heavy vehicle, moves forward with slow and heavy strides. Urged to greater speed, he rolls his shoulders so that it is almost impossible to rise to his trot. When put to the canter he pounds along the road, his hind-feet kept far in the rear and his head swaying up and down, while, missing the customary support of the bearing-rein, he all the time leans his heavy head on his rider's delicate arm, till it seems as if she would be pulled out of the saddle. However, the fresh open air is there, and the scenery; exercise, too, in plenty, and the pleasure of independent movement, so that our heroine is half inclined to persevere. But, alas! an equestrian party on well-bitted, light-stepping horses sweeps by, casting a pitying glance at her rustic mount and helpless plight. Mortified and discouraged, she goes home and dismounts, determined not to try again. Nevertheless, her horse is very likely quite as good as theirs, and all he wants is a little "handling," as the horsemen say. For twenty-five dollars a riding-master will turn him over to her as docile and supple as any of them, and, with a little time and trouble, she can do it herself for nothing.

As for the proficiency in riding requisite, it is only necessary that you should not depend upon the reins for your balance—a common habit, but one destructive of all delicacy of the horse's mouth.

As the first half-dozen lessons of this course are to be given on foot, a riding-habit would only be in the way; so go to your first *tête-à-tête* with your new scholar in a stout walking-dress, easy in the waist, short of skirt, and of stuff that will bear scouring, for frothy lips will certainly be wiped on it. Let the hat be trim, the gloves strong and old, and the boots heavy with low heels.

The saddle should, if possible, be of the safe and easy modern pattern, with hunting-horn and low pommel on the right side—but of course any one which does not gall the horse can be made to do. It should have at least two strong girths, and must be so padded with wool as not to touch the backbone. Make sure, before putting it on, that there are no tacks loose or likely to become so in the lining.

The bridle should be a double one, with one "snaffle" or jointed bit, and one curb-bit, each having, of course, separate reins and headstalls. By-and-by you can use a single bridle, if you prefer, with whichever bit you think best suited to your hand and your horse's mouth.

The whip should be elastic and capable of giving a sharp cut (though you may never need to administer one with it), and it is convenient to have a loop of cord or ribbon by which it may be hung to the wrist. A good birch switch is better for your present purpose than the usual flimsy "lady's whip;" and if you are in

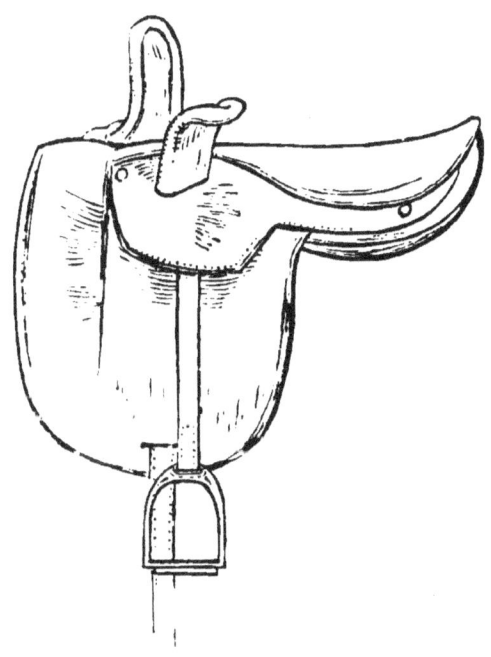

A GOOD SADDLE.

the country, it makes a good whip to begin with, as you will probably soon wish to substitute a crop.

The place of instruction should be as retired as possible, so that there may be nothing to distract the horse's attention.

For the first few lessons it will be well, if you are not thoroughly at home with horses, to have a man—some friend or attendant—near at hand to give you confidence by his presence, and to come to your aid in case of necessity.

LESSON I.

COMING TO THE WHIP.

Have the horse brought saddled and bridled. Walk quietly up in front of him, with your riding-whip under your arm, and look him kindly in the face. See that the bridle fits properly, as a careless groom may have neglected to adjust it to the length of the head.

The *throat-latch* should be loose enough to permit the chin to come easily to the breast; the bits should lie in their proper place on the *bars*, and the curb-chain should lie flat in the *chin groove*, just tight enough to allow your fore-finger to pass under it. The *bars* are that part of the gum between the *grinders*, or back teeth, and the *nippers*, or front teeth, which in the mare is destitute of teeth, and in the horse has a tusk called the *bridle-tooth*.

It is upon these bars, of course, that the bits should lie, and the curb-bit, according to military rule, at an inch above the tusk. By general usage they are placed too high, the proper place of the curb-bit being not up in the corner of the lips, but opposite or nearly opposite the chin groove, which is just above the swell of the lower lip. If the curb-chain is too loose the bit will "fall through," or turn around in the mouth. If it is too tight, or is ill adjusted, or if, from the bits being too high, it slips up where the skin is thinner and the bones sharper, it will give such pain that, to avoid it, the nose will be thrust out instead of being brought in. The chain should press below the snaffle, or the latter will

A PROPERLY FITTED CURB-CHAIN.

unhook it. Adjust and settle the various straps with your hand, speaking kindly to your horse at the same time; but when you have begun to teach him, reserve all praises and caresses to reward him when he has done well. It is a good plan to give him a lump of sugar before you begin and after you finish each lesson.

Now, standing in front of the horse, take both curb-reins in the left hand at six inches below the bit, and, with the whip held tip downward in the right hand, strike him a light blow on the breast; in about a second give him another, and continue striking at the same interval, looking calmly at him the while, and following him if he steps backward or sideways.

Sooner or later, and usually very soon, he will come straight towards you; then instantly relax his head, say "Bravo! bravo!" and stroke him on the face and neck. You will very likely hear him give a deep sigh of relief, like a frightened child. Give him half a minute or more, according to circumstances, to look about and recover from his nervousness — for you will find that his nerves work a good deal like your own — and then begin again, allowing him after every trial a half-minute or so of rest.

It will not be long before he discovers that the way to avoid the whip is to come straight to you, and he will do so at the least motion of it. Take advantage of this to make him curve his neck, put his head in the proper perpendicular position, and bring his haunches under him, by holding him back with the curb-reins as he presses towards you. This lesson, to a careless observer, looks rather pretty than useful, but is indispensable for your purpose, for it gives you the means of preventing the horse from backing while you are teaching him the flexions of the jaw and of the neck. It shows him, also, that the whip is only to be dreaded when he disobeys, so that later on it will become in your hands, strange as it may now seem to you, a powerful means of calming his ardor and soothing his impatience, and thus sparing your bridle-hand the sometimes excessive fatigue of restraining his impetuosity.

In practice it is not necessary to carry this instruction to the point where the horse will come to you from so great a distance as shown in the accompanying cut, though there is no difficulty in so doing.

A certain English nobleman used to say that a man was as much above his ordinary self on horseback as he was at other times above the brutes. Possibly more than one young equestrian, remembering the exhilaration of some morning ride, the quickened appreciation, the redoubled enjoyment of the beauties of nature, and of the charm of congenial companionship, will be ready to echo the sentiment. It is only true, however, even approximately, *when the rider controls all the forces of the horse*, and it is the object of the present article to put this perfect control within the reach of every one willing to take the time and trouble to acquire it, for not daring, but calmness, not strength, but perseverance, are the qualities requisite.

Both time and trouble undoubtedly will be required, for while, by even a careless use of this method, your horse may be made vastly more comfortable under the saddle, yet only by tact and patience can you win that mastery over his every volition by which his splendid strength, courage, and endurance will seem to be added to your own. You will find him, however, no tiresome pupil. On the contrary, every day will increase your pleasure both in his progress and in his companionship, for he will soon become attached to you, and will now and then turn his head and look at you with such an expression in his eyes that you will think the old belief in the transmigration of souls not so very wonderful after all. You will, besides, find in your lessons no contemptible discipline of character, for you will have to conquer your natural timidity in feeling your weakness opposed to his strength, to suppress your impatience when he is slow of apprehension, to remain calm when he is restive, and to award him your caresses, not because his neck is sleek and beautiful, but because he has done exactly as you directed. You will find also that they will have a tendency to improve your seat, by taking your attention from yourself, and with it some of the involuntary stiffness always born of self-consciousness.

A different, but equally practical, result of knowing something of horse-training is that wherever you may be you will have no difficulty in getting a mount— no small advantage either, as many an enthusiastic young girl can testify as she remembers the stony look which came over some comfortable farmer's countenance when she confidingly asked to ride one of his round-bellied horses. Many an owner of a trained saddle-horse would gladly have him ridden carefully by one capable of keeping him "in good form," while every horse-owner, no matter how poor his nags, dreads an ignorant rider as he does the epizooty. Probably scores of country stable-keepers and thousands of farmers, after a season's experience with ordinary city riders, have vowed never to let a woman mount one of their horses again. One of the former, at a popular summer resort, said to the writer, "Two ladies hurt my hosses more last summer than all the rest of the work. They ain't no more saddles to be found in my stable!" A neighboring farmer, who had at first thought to reap a golden harvest from his five excellent horses at a dollar a ride, hereupon remarked, "They hain't no sense. They think a horse will go like a machine, and all they've got to do is to turn steam on with the whip." Very different would have been the verdict had the riders but possessed even a slight experience in training, for the horses would have come from their hands improved in mouth and gait, and almost certainly uninjured by bad usage.

LESSON II.

TO HOLD THE BIT LIGHTLY (*FLEXION DE LA MÂCHOIRE*), USING THE CURB.

BEGIN by assuring yourself that the horse has forgotten nothing of the previous lesson. Do not allow him to sidle up to you upon your movement of the whip towards him, nor to twist his nose towards you, but make him advance in a straight line.

Now, standing at the left of the horse's head, with your feet firmly planted a little way apart, take the left snaffle-rein in the left hand, and the left curb-rein in the right, at five or six inches from their respective bits, and having brought the head into the proper perpendicular position, pull the two hands apart with gentle but steady force. Hold your whip, meanwhile, tip downward in the right hand, to prevent him from running back, which can be done without relaxing your pull by tapping him with it upon the breast.

The object of this lesson, as well as of those which follow, is to overcome involuntary muscular contraction. In some cases, as probably in the present one, the contractions are simply nervous, and will cease with the mental cause; in others the muscles have grown into improper positions, so that time will be required to set them right.

Your object at present is to get the jaw relaxed, so that you can move it at pleasure without resistance, and

FLEXION OF THE JAW—USING THE CURB.

this may take time and patience, for you must not be satisfied with anything less than complete success, or you will repent it later. At first, however, seize the slightest involuntary opening of the horse's mouth as an excuse to relax your hold, caress and praise him, then let him stand a half-minute with his head free, and begin again.

When he is submissive, and pleased with you, he will almost always show it by gently champing his bit; but do not be deceived by a nervous simulation which you will probably detect, and which consists in opening the mouth a very little and immediately gripping the bit again. You will have been completely successful when, by simply drawing on the curb-reins, the head is brought to the proper perpendicular position, and the bit, instead of being gripped, is held lightly in the mouth, or, to use the school term, when the horse is " light in hand."

This is the only lesson in the series in which it is possible (though not probable) that your unaided strength may be insufficient; if so, get some one to help you over the first resistance of the horse. With care and tact, however, you will in all probability require no assistance.

LESSON III.

TO HOLD THE BIT LIGHTLY, USING THE SNAFFLE.

Begin by repeating in proper order all that has been done at the previous lessons. Now, having got the horse "light in hand" with the curb, relax the curb-rein and try to keep him light with the snaffle.

He will probably begin to bear on it. If so, restrain him by successive tugs, punishing him a little with the curb, if necessary, and always rewarding him with praises and caresses when he does well. Avoid any violent use of the curb, or the horse, in his efforts to escape the pain, may get his tongue over the bit, and thus acquire a very troublesome habit. It must be remembered that the bit being the principal channel of communication between his mind and yours, his whole attention is concentrated upon it, and he is almost as much disconcerted by a sudden harsh movement of it as you would be by an unexpected shout in your ear.

By this time your groom is perhaps watching you with interest, and may be trusted to repeat your handling, thus saving you some time and trouble; but, as a general thing, two lessons a day of from half to three-quarters of an hour each, are as much as a horse can receive with profit.

LESSON IV.

TO LOWER THE HEAD.

ALWAYS look over your horse before beginning your instruction, to see that he has not met with any mishap. Observe that his eye is bright and that he feels in good spirits; run your eye over his limbs to detect any cut, bruise, or swelling; see that the hoofs are not cracked.

Assure yourself that he is properly groomed — one good test being the absence of scurf at the roots of the mane; that his mouth has been sponged out before putting in the bit, his hoofs wiped off clean — never, however, blacked — and that he is properly saddled and bridled. With a little practice you will do all this in half a minute, while you are buttoning your gloves. About once a week ask after his food and appetite, and make the groom show you his shoes; and when the time comes for him to be re-shod (which should be at least once a month) positively forbid any trimming of the frog or of the inside of the hoof — any "cleaning up of the foot," as farriers are pleased to call it. The only part to be touched with the knife is the bottom of the outer, horny shell, which is not half an inch thick; and even this

LOWERING THE HEAD.

must be cut with moderation, never burned by fitting the shoe to it hot—the common makeshift of lazy farriers—nor filed on the outside, as both these operations not only weaken the hoof but impair Nature's arrangement for oiling and lubricating it. Should the horse not bear equal weight on all four legs, move him a step to see if the faulty posture may not have been acci-

TO LOWER THE HEAD. 27

PUNISHMENT IN CASE OF RESISTANCE.

dental; and if it is repeated, examine the "favored" leg, carefully laying your bare hand on the hoof and joints to detect inflammation, feeling along the bones for lumps, comparing any suspicious spot with the same part of the corresponding leg, observing whether it is warmer or more sensitive than its fellow.

Having assured yourself that your horse is in perfect

order, and that he has forgotten nothing of your previous instruction, you will now proceed to the lesson of the day. Place yourself on his left, or "near," side, take the snaffle-reins at a few inches from the bit, and pull his head downward. Should he not yield, cross the reins, by taking the right rein in the left hand and *vice versa*, which will pinch his jaw sharply, and pull again till he drops his head, when you will hold it down a few seconds, praising him the while; then raise it up, and allow him a little time to rest.

For our young readers we give below a few of the more usual technical terms, of which it will be found convenient to have a knowledge in the course of these lessons:

Amble.—A gait like pacing, but slower, in which the two legs on the same side are moved together.

Appel.—The gentle tug on the rein given by the horse at each step.

Arrière-main.—That part of the horse back of the saddle, called, not quite correctly, in this article, the *croup.*

Avant-main.—That part of the horse forward of the saddle—the forehand.

Bore.—To lean on the bit.

Bridle-tooth.—Tusk found in the horse's mouth, though not in the mare's, between nippers and grinders.

Bucking.—Leaping vertically into the air with all four feet at once.

Chin Groove.—That part of underjaw next the swell of lower lip in which curb-chain rests.

Curb.—Bit without joint, with levers at side and chain, which, passing under jaw, serves as a fulcrum to communicate pressure of bit to bars of mouth.

Deux Pistes.—To go on *deux pistes* is to advance with the body placed obliquely, so that the hind feet move on a different line or *piste* from the fore.

Elbow.—Joint of fore-leg next above knee, lying next horse's side.

Fetlock.—Joint next below knee.

Forearm.—That part of leg between elbow and knee.

Forge.—To strike the toe of the fore-foot with the toe of the hind-foot—usually the result of bad shoeing.

Frog.—Triangular piece of spongy horn in middle of sole of foot, forming a cushion for the navicular bone.

Grinders.—Back teeth.

Hand.—Four inches (one-third of a foot).

Hand-gallop.—A slow gallop.

Haute École—Haut Manége.—The complete course of training given in the French military riding-schools. To translate this by "high-school," as is sometimes done, produces a ludicrous impression.

Hock.—Joint of hind-leg between thigh and shank.

Interfere.—To strike the fetlock with the foot—often caused by bad shoeing.

Manége.—Horse-training, also the training-school itself.

Nippers.—Front teeth.

Pace.—A rapid gait, in which the fore and hind foot on same side move at same time and strike the ground together.

Pastern.—Bones between fetlock and foot.

Passage.—Moving sideways, as to close up or open the ranks, as in cavalry exercises.

Pirouette.—Wheeling on the hind-legs.

Pirouette renversée.—Wheeling on the fore-legs.

Piaffer.—A slow and cadenced trot, in which the horse balances a certain time on each pair of feet.

Piste.—The imaginary circle (usually, however, a well-beaten track) three feet from the wall of the *manége*.

Poll.—Top of head between the ears.

Rack.—A gait somewhat similar to *single-foot*.

Ramener.—To bring the head to the perpendicular.

Rassembler.—To get the horse together, with his legs well under him and his head perpendicular.

Shank.—Parts of fore-leg between knee and fetlock, and parts of hind-leg between hock and fetlock.

Single-foot.—A very rapid gait, taught principally in the Western States of America, in which one foot is put down at a time.

Snaffle.—Bit jointed in middle, without side levers or chin-chain.

Spavins and *Splints.*—Excrescences on bones of legs, usually caused by strain. When they occur on the fore-shanks they are called splints, and may do no harm.

If on the hind-legs they are called spavins, and usually result in permanent lameness.

Stifle.—Joint of hind-leg between hip and hock, lying against horse's side.

Surcingle.— A girth extending entirely around the horse.

Thigh. — Popularly speaking, it comprises the two upper joints of hind-leg from hip to hock.

Throat-latch.—That strap of the bridle which passes under the throat.

Withers.—Highest point of shoulder between neck and saddle.

LESSON V.

TO BEND THE NECK TO RIGHT AND LEFT, WITH THE REINS HELD BELOW THE BIT (*FLEXIONS DE L'ENCOLURE*).

BEFORE beginning each lesson it is well, as has been already recommended, to review hastily the instruction previously given.

Now place yourself on the left side of your horse, with your riding-whip tip downward in your right hand, and with your feet firmly planted a little apart. Take the right curb-rein in your right hand at about six inches from the lever of the bit, and the left curb-rein in your left at three inches from the lever, and having brought the horse's head to a perpendicular position, pull the two hands steadily apart, moving the right hand to the right and the left hand to the left, so as to pry the horse's head around to the right by means of the twist of the bit in his mouth. If he offers to back, stop him by tapping his breast with the whip; if he tries to pull away his head, hold on tight, until presently he will turn his head to the right, when you will instantly say, "Bravo! bravo!" and after holding it so a few seconds, bring it back to its original position. Very soon he will take the idea, and you will bring his head around until it faces backward, being careful to keep it always exactly perpendicular, and not to allow the horse to move it of his own accord in any direction.

Now try to obtain this flexion with the right-hand rein alone, only using the left hand to assist it if he fails

"PULLING THE HANDS STEADILY APART."

to understand or to obey, and also to bring back the head to its original position.

To bend the neck to the left requires simply a reversal of the process just described, and will give you probably no trouble. Do not be satisfied with anything else than an easy, graceful, and patient obedience on the part of the horse. Should he back or fidget out of his place, bring him back to it before going on, as you will find that his associations (unconscious, doubtless) with place are remarkable, and that any fault is likely to be repeated on the spot where it was first committed.

TO BEND THE NECK TO RIGHT OR LEFT, WITH THE REINS BELOW THE BITS.

When he will look backward on either side, and remain looking so upon your drawing upon the proper rein, the lesson is perfect. The utility of it may not appear at first, but will be evident at a later stage of your instructions.

LESSON VI.

TO BEND THE NECK TO RIGHT AND LEFT, WITH THE REINS THROWN OVER THE NECK.

TAKE the left snaffle-rein in the left hand at about a foot from the bit, and with the right hand draw the right snaffle-rein over the horse's neck just in front of the shoulder, until both sides pull equally on the bit

GETTING THE HORSE "LIGHT IN HAND."

and the horse is "light in hand." Then, by drawing upon the right rein gradually, bend his head around to the right, gently feeling the left rein so as to keep the bit straight in the mouth and prevent him from moving

PULLING ON THE RIGHT REIN.

faster than you wish; for in this, as in all other cases, while he is to do exactly what you direct, he is to do nothing more.

To bend the neck to the left, you will, of course, reverse the operation above described, standing on the other side of the horse, taking the right snaffle-rein in the right hand at a foot from the bit, and drawing the left rein over the shoulder with the left hand. Keep the horse "light in hand" all the time, and his head perfectly perpendicular, as any twisting of the nose to one side has a ludicrous appearance. Now repeat with the curb.

LESSON VII.

TO MOVE THE CROUP TO RIGHT AND LEFT WITH THE WHIP.

It is unfortunate that we have not in English a vocabulary of definite terms relating to the training and riding of horses. We will for convenience call all that part of the horse in front of the saddle the *forehand*, and all that part back of the saddle the *croup*.

Take both snaffle-reins in the left hand at a few inches from the bit, and standing near the horse's left shoulder, get him "light in hand" with the bit; and if his hind-legs are not well under him, make him bring them forward by tapping him gently on the rump with your extended whip, keeping the forehand motionless by your hold on the bit.

Now, holding his head so that he will not move his left fore-foot, tap him lightly on the left flank near the hip until he moves the croup one step to the right.

Then pat and praise him, and if he has not moved his right fore-foot, tap his right leg with the whip to make him bring it forward even with the left. After a little rest begin again, asking and allowing only one step at a time, and persevering until he will move the croup one step over to each tap of the whip, pivoting on the left fore-foot and walking the right foot by little steps around it.

MOVING THE CROUP ONE STEP TO THE RIGHT.

When he is perfect with the snaffle, repeat the process with the curb, keeping his hind-legs well under him, and holding him "light in hand," while maintaining his left fore-foot immovable, with a delicate touch, to resemble as much as possible the action of the rein when drawn from the saddle.

Now repeat the process to the left, taking your stand

near the right shoulder, and, with both snaffle-reins in your right hand and the whip in your left, proceed as before until the horse will walk one step at each tap of the whip around the right fore-foot, which should in its turn be kept so firmly in place as to bore a hole in the ground. Repeat with the curb.

This lesson, which will last, very likely, two or three days, may appear to some of no practical utility, but it is indispensable alike to your comfort when mounted, to the safety of those who accompany or meet you, and to the continued education of your horse. Who has not seen an untrained animal force his rider to dismount to lift some gate-latch which was really within easy reach, or prancing about in a crowd, to the terror and vexation of his neighbors, or in momentary danger of hooking his legs into the wheels of passing vehicles?

Now, if you trample on any one, or upset a light vehicle, though you risk, and perhaps break, your own bones, yet you are liable for damages; and this fact is so well known that a suit will be promptly begun against you. Besides, for your own sake you must have it in your power to get your horse's haunches, and with them your own person, out of danger from careless or mischievous drivers—just as a cavalryman has to save his horse from a slash or thrust.

LESSON VIII.
MOUNTED.

To Advance at Touch of Heel and Stop at Touch of Whip on Back.—Your horse's education must now be carried on from the saddle, and should he never have been ridden, it will be prudent to have a man mount him first upon a man's saddle, and afterwards upon your side-saddle, with a blanket wrapped around the legs to simulate a skirt. If the previous lessons have been carefully given, you will have no trouble in making him stand wherever you please while you mount, nor in getting him "light in hand" afterwards. First, however, see that the saddle fits snugly in its place, and that the girths are good and in order. If there are more than two, let the third be loose while the others are tight. The writer once saw a powerful horse burst two good English girths by a sudden bound and throw off his rider, saddle and all. If the girths and saddle are not very strong, put a broad, thin strap—a surcingle will do—over all.

Being mounted, gather the reins all into the left hand in the following manner: Draw the right snaffle-rein between the fore and middle fingers, and the left snaffle rein under the little finger into the palm, throwing the ends forward together over the first finger, to be held by the thumb; in like manner draw the curb-reins into the palm on each side of the ring-finger, the left

GETTING A HORSE ACCUSTOMED TO SKIRTS.
(An example of the "flying trot.")

rein, of course, below, and the right above it, throwing the ends, like those of the snaffle, forward over the forefinger and under the thumb. Now taking the curb-rein by the seam, draw it through your fingers till both reins fall equally on the bit; then do the same by the snaffle, but draw it so much tighter than the curb that the latter will hang loose, and any movement of your hand will be felt through the snaffle. Grasp all the reins firmly, your hand back upward, with wrist a little bent and elbow near your side, so that if the horse, stumbling, thrust his nose suddenly out, you will not be jerked from the saddle.

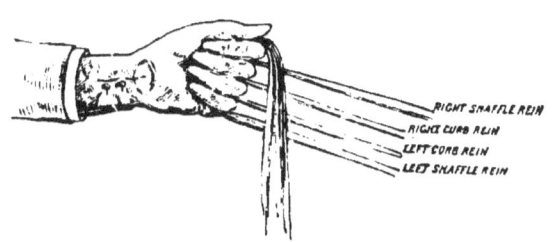

SHOWING REINS IN LEFT HAND.

All this you will quickly get the knack of, and do as easily as you would thread a needle. You will observe that, having the width of three fingers between the two snaffle-reins, you can, by bending your wrist to right or left, guide the horse as easily as with the reins in both hands. Get the horse "light in hand" by the usual play of the bit, first the curb, then the snaffle, tapping him on the right side, just forward of the girth, if he fails to respond or offers to back.

Now press him just back of the girth with your left heel, at the same time relaxing the rein a little. If he steps forward, pat and praise him, but if not, press him more firmly, at the same time touching him as before with the whip. When he moves forward praise him, and after a few seconds stop him, leaning back a little and laying your whip by a turn of the wrist on his back just behind the saddle. Then recommence, and persevere until he will start promptly forward at the touch of the heel, and stop at the touch of the whip on his back, keeping "light in hand" the while. If he is very

ADVANCING AT TOUCH OF HEEL.

sluggish you may have to strike him smartly for not answering instantly to the heel, but he will soon learn not to wait for the blow. Let the heel act close to the girth, as you will soon wish to move the croup over by the same means applied farther back. It is well not to start with the whip, nor by chirping or clucking, which

STOPPING AT TOUCH OF WHIP ON BACK.

is as likely to excite your companion's horse as your own, and is annoying to most people.

Accustom your horse to stop short, whether at the pull on the reins, the touch of the whip, or the word "Whoa."

After riding have the saddle removed, and should a puffy spot appear on the back where it has pressed, take the hint at once and have the padding eased over the place, or a tedious and vexatious "saddle-gall" may result. There is no better treatment for such a spot than bathing with very hot water. As a preventive, however, it is an excellent plan to bathe the back with cold water, afterwards carefully rubbing dry.

The several instruments of torture represented in the

THE WALK (COLT IN TRAINING).

above cut are the *dumb-jockey* upon the horse's back, the *cavesson* around his nose, and the *lunging-cord* in the hands of the groom—to whom the artist has very properly given the countenance of one who, had he lived in old times, would have lent a hand at the rack or the iron boot without wincing. The dumb-jockey has elastic reins, which are adjusted so as to hold the head in the proper position. The cavesson is a broad leather band, stiffened with iron, which is fastened around the nose just where the cartilage joins the bone, so that a tug upon it causes great pain, and will bring anything but determined vice to submission. These appliances are usually only the resort of laziness or ignorance, for none of them can for a moment compare with the human hand; and in fact they effect no saving in time, for it is not safe to leave a horse a minute alone with a dumb-jockey on his back, as he may rear and fall over backward at the risk of his life. The writer knew of an accident of this kind which ended the victim's usefulness in the saddle, and he has seen a strong and proud horse sweat profusely, with the thermometer at ten degrees below the freezing point, while being *lunged, i. e.*, driven in a ring, with a dumb-jockey on.

LESSON IX.

MOUNTED.

To Bend the Neck to Right and Left. — You can now, if you please, substitute a stiff *crop* for the flexible whip you have so far made use of. Having taken your place in the saddle and got your horse light in hand review the previous lesson; then, having your horse still carefully light in hand and light on foot — that is, with hind-feet well under him — draw gently upon the left snaffle-rein. When the horse's head has come around to your knee, keep it in that position an instant, and then put it straight again by drawing upon the right rein, insisting that his face remains perpendicular during the whole operation. Now go through the same process with the right snaffle-rein, and then repeat the whole operation with the curb. These flexions of the neck may now seem to you of doubtful utility, but as the education of the horse advances, your opinion will change. It is as rare for horses as for people to have a noble and graceful carriage; and while you cannot, of course, really change the shape of your mount, yet you can, by care, entirely change his appear-

BENDING THE NECK TO RIGHT AND LEFT.

ance. His various gaits you can indeed improve, but for his *style* he depends, nine times out of ten, entirely upon you, and if you are indifferent he will be careless and probably clumsy.

LESSON X.

THE WALK.

This gait is apt to be hardly appreciated by youthful equestrians, whose love of excitement leads them often to prefer rapidity to grace of motion; but it can, with a little painstaking, be made swift and agreeable; and certainly, when light and animated, it shows off both horse and rider to better advantage than any other. It is, besides, an indispensable stage in the bitting of the horse; for until he will continue "light" while starting, stopping, and turning at a walk, he should not be put to a faster pace.

Your chief difficulty will be his propensity to drop into a jog-trot as soon as you try to quicken his steps; but this must be overcome by stopping him immediately and then recommencing the walk, urging him forward with the heel and encouraging him to lift his feet quickly by a delicate play of the bit, but leaving his head as free as possible. This will give you occupation, probably, for several days. Do not forget to praise him when he does well.

LESSON XI.
TO MOVE THE CROUP WITH HEEL AND WHIP (*PIROUETTE RENVERSÉE*).

Having your horse light in hand and light on foot (that is to say, as we have before explained, with his face perpendicular, the bit held lightly, and his weight well supported on his hind-legs), tap him on the right flank with your whip or "crop" till he moves the croup one step to the left. Your great difficulty will be to prevent him from moving his right fore-foot, which by careful play of the bit you must endeavor to keep fixed to the ground, while at each tap of the whip the other three feet move one step around it. When this lesson has been satisfactorily learned, proceed to teach in like manner the movement of croup to the right, pivoting on the left fore-foot, substituting, however, for the tap of the whip a pressure with the left heel, applied as far behind the girth as possible.

Should he not understand this pressure, interpret it to him with the whip. As long as there seems to be any mental effort required on his part, pause after each step to caress and praise him. Be careful to keep him

TO MOVE THE CROUP WITH HEEL AND WHIP. 53

MOVING THE CROUP WITH THE HEEL AND WHIP.

calm while learning, or he may tread one foot upon the other, possibly inflicting a severe wound, and after dismounting inspect his feet carefully to make sure that this has not happened.

LESSON XII.

TO GUIDE "BRIDLEWISE."

Up to this time your horse has been guided as in driving, by a pull upon one side of the bit, that is to say, upon one corner of the mouth, and it is time now to substitute a simple pressure of the rein upon his neck. The chief difficulty to be encountered is in the fact that, as the rein is attached to the bit, the tension of it against one side of the neck pulls the bit on that side, consequently conveying to the horse an impression exactly opposite to that intended. This difficulty must be overcome by patience, for this instruction cannot be completed in a single lesson, but will have to be carried on simultaneously with other work for a week or more. It is given by carrying your hand over, whenever you turn, to the side towards which you wish to go, so that the reins will press against the neck. Thus, if you wish to turn to the left, draw on the left snaffle-rein, and as the horse answers to it, carry your hand to the left, so that the right reins press against the right side of the neck. This must be done with judgment, or the bit, being pulled too hard on the right side by the tension of the rein on the neck, will stop him in his turn. Of course you will seek as many occasions as possible for turning, choosing, in preference, places where your intention cannot be misunderstood, as at a corner, for instance. There is no better spot than some old orchard, for the horse instantly takes the idea of going

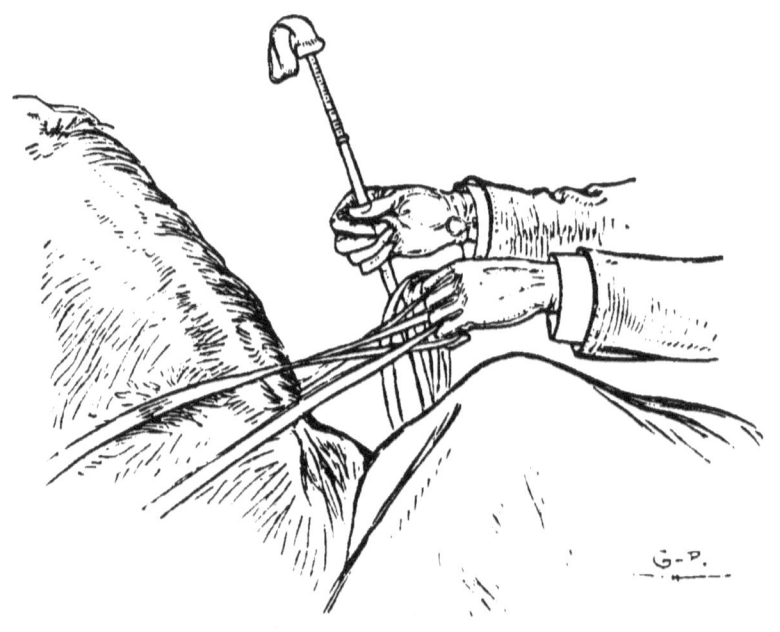

GUIDING BRIDLEWISE (TURNING TO THE RIGHT).

around a tree, and there will be more or less shade, and probably good turf. While he is learning this lesson do not distract his attention by other instruction; but as soon as he has mastered it, see that his head is always turned in the direction towards which he is to go, for it is a habit with horses, as awkward as it is common, to turn one way and look the other. At the same time always lean in your saddle towards the centre of the curve you are describing, and at an angle increasing in proportion to your speed.

Some English writers depreciate the above method of guiding the horse, preferring to use the bit exclusively, but it is almost universal in the United States, and its advantages for ordinary riders are numerous and evident. Indeed, Stonehenge, a well-known English authority, says that in "this way a horse can be turned with a much greater degree of nicety and smoothness than by acting on the corner of his mouth."

LESSON XIII.
THE TROT.

Writers on the horse distinguish three kinds of trot, *viz.*, the "jog" trot, the "true" trot, and the "flying" or "American" trot. In the first the feet remain longer on the ground than in the air, and lazy animals are naturally fond of it, while spirited horses sometimes drop into it from impatience of walking. It is, however, apt to be a slovenly gait, which, though easy to the rider, should hardly be permitted.

In the flying trot the horse leaps a considerable distance through the air at each stride—evidently a mode of progression unsuited for ladies, who must attain speed in trotting by quickening the step without undue lengthening of the stride.

Your first care will be to prevent your horse from losing his "lightness," as he will be inclined to do at every change of gait or increase of speed—and this, while often by no means easy, is yet a task to be thoroughly accomplished if you wish for comfort or style in the future. You will observe in trotting, as in all other gaits, at each step a slight tug on the rein, called by some writers the *appel*, and this you will ordinarily yield your hand to, so as to keep a steady feeling of the mouth.

If, however, the horse begins to bear on the bit, hold your hand firmly, with the rein just so tight that at every step he will himself thrust his jaw against the curb. This will very likely bring him to his senses and restore his lightness, and if so, pat and praise him; but if not, tap him on the side with your whip, at the same time pulling on the curb for a second or two. If he does not yield to this, repeated two or three times, stop him short; and when, by the same method, you have got him to relax his gripe of the bit and arch his neck, allow him to go on again. He will dislike excessively to be stopped and started in this way, and when he finds that he will not be permitted to go in any way but the right one he will give up the attempt.

Do not try to succeed by giving a long, steady pull, nor by using force, as it will do no good, and may cause the tongue to be put over the bit—a very troublesome trick. Remember, in stopping, to lean back, and lay your whip, by a movement of the wrist, on the horse's back.

You will next turn your attention to your horse's gait. As the trot is rarely so easy that a lady can sit down to it with comfort, it is advisable to rise in the stirrup.

This is difficult and fatiguing if the stride is too long,

and you will therefore prevent its extending too much by giving a little tug on the rein just as each step is made, at the same time with the heel keeping up speed and animation.

If your bitting has been thoroughly done, and your horse's mouth is fine and sensitive, you will probably find the snaffle best for trotting, and you will give a steady support with it.

Keep the step quick, elastic, perfectly cadenced, and without any rolling of the shoulders.

Should you happen to be mounted upon a horse which, from bad handling or his own faulty conformation, is disposed to "bore," or bear on his bit, you will ride with the curb, taking its reins in one hand, but in the other hand taking the snaffle, with the left rein drawn much tighter than the right. This will have an effect quite different from what one might expect, and will put a stop to this most fatiguing and annoying trick.

This recipe is not found in Baucher's book, but is said to have been given by him verbally to his pupils, and it is really "a trick worth knowing." If it does not have the desired effect, however, when practised with the left snaffle-rein, try it with the right, as the mouth—for instance, from the effect of double harness—may not be equally sensitive on both sides.

If you observe that the step of one foot is shorter than that of the other, making the horse appear lame, you may be almost sure you have fallen into the too common feminine practice of bearing too much of your weight on one side. An even balance in the saddle is of capital importance, and a rough-and-ready test is to observe whether the buttons of your habit are in the same plane as the horse's backbone, and your shoulders nearly equidistant from his ears—points of which you can judge as well as any one.

In the matter of the horse's gait you must be equally exacting, not resting so long as you can perceive the slightest irregularity or difference between the strides. It is desirable to cultivate such a sensitiveness to all the horse's movements as will enable you to know where his feet are at all times without looking, and the first step towards this is to learn to "sit close to the saddle." This firm and easy seat, coveted by every rider, is attained by some with much greater difficulty than by others. Many riders will bump about on their saddles for thousands of miles without being "shaken into their seat," because they neither abandon themselves to the instinct which correctly guides a child, nor, on the other hand, seek out and remove the cause, in the muscular contractions of the body and limbs.

A loose sack of grain set upright on horseback does not jump up and down, and, while it is not desirable to be quite so inert as a bag of grain, yet a lesson may be learned from it—which is, that the lower part of the person, from the hips to the knees, should be kept firmly and steadily, though not stiffly, in place, while the waist, with the back bent slightly inward, should be as flexible as possible, and the whole upper part of the person pliant and supple, so as to yield with a certain *nonchalance* to every movement.

Nervous riders, like nervous horses, are those in whom involuntary muscular contractions persist the most obstinately.

As both of the horse's strides are equal when the trot is true, it seems nonsense to talk, as some writers do, about the "leading foot" in trotting; and except that few horses are so perfectly symmetrical that both strides are equally elastic, there should be no difference to a man on which one he "rises," and he will therefore spare that foot and leg which, for any cause, he may suppose to be the weaker. A lady will without effort find the stride best suited to her.

Horses are often trained in our Western States to trot when the rider touches the back of their neck, and to single-foot or pace when he makes play gently with the curb-bit. These signals are injudicious, because in harness a slight movement of the bit sets the horse so trained to single-footing, and there is no way to communicate to him your wish that he should trot. It is better, therefore, to give the signal to trot by taking a firm hold of the snaffle, and laying your whip gently on his hind-quarter while you incite to speed with your heel.

After dismounting, observe whether your horse has *interfered*—that is, struck one or more of his fetlock joints with his hoofs; should the skin be knocked off, apply some healing ointment; and if the joint swells, bathe with water as hot as the hand will bear. This is the best remedy for all ordinary bruises and sprains.

LESSON XIV.
THE GALLOP, HAND-GALLOP, AND CANTER.

These are treated of by some writers as distinct, the canter being called "purely artificial;" but it will be convenient and sufficiently accurate for our purpose to take them up together and to consider the canter as what it in fact is—an *improved*, and not an "artificial," gait. Horses undoubtedly often canter in a rude way without being taught, as may be seen often in the field, and not seldom in harness, and you will probably have little trouble in getting your horse to do the same. It is this natural canter which is called by country people the "lope." It is of importance, however, that your horse should not change his gait without orders, no matter how hard pressed, this being especially true if he is to be driven as well as ridden. The signal to canter should, therefore, be such as can be given only from the saddle. It is well not to use the whip for the purpose, but to try by raising the bridle to lift the forehand, while stimulating at the same time with the heel. Should he persist in trotting, do not get vexed or discouraged, for he is only resisting temptation to

THE CANTER.

do what he has expressly been taught not to do; but continue your incitements, raising the bridle-hand firmly at every stride till you have got him fairly off his feet into a gallop, when you will soothe his nerves by patting and praising him, and gradually calm him down into a canter, lifting your hand at every stride to prevent his relapsing into a trot. When he will canter promptly at the signal, you will get him "light in hand" before giving it; then make him start without thrusting out his nose, and keep him light by the means already detailed in the lesson on the trot. Next you will bring his haunches forward under him, which is the great point, and increase the brilliancy of his action by stimulating him with heel and whip, while at each step you restrain him by a gentle pull, so that he will not spring forward so far as he intended. Persevere until he will canter as slowly as he would walk. Your best guide will be to observe the action of some well-trained and well-ridden horse, and to endeavor to obtain the same in yours.

To *change the leading foot* in cantering is, however, a more difficult matter, and we will postpone the consideration of it until his education is a little farther advanced. In the mean time you will avoid turning a sharp corner at a canter.

The hand-gallop is simply a moderate gallop in which the ear observes three beats,

as in the canter, but swifter; while in the extended gallop it hears but two,

though given with a sort of rattle, which shows that

neither the fore nor the hind feet strike the ground exactly together, as they do in leaping.

Keep to the left, as the law directs, is an admonition on bridges and other thoroughfares in England which has often excited the surprise of Americans, very likely eliciting some such comment as "How stupid!" "How perfectly ridiculous!" Yet for many centuries it was really the only safe way to turn, whether on foot or on horseback, and as all our fashions of riding and driving are based upon it, it is hard to see why the custom should have changed in this country. In the olden time, when people went about principally on horseback, when roads were lonely and footpads plenty, it would have been "perfectly ridiculous" for a man to turn to the right and expose his defenceless bridle-arm to a blow from a bludgeon or slash from a hanger. Much more would it have been so had he a lady under his care, who would thus be left in the very front of danger, whether it might be of robbery from highwaymen, of insult from roistering riders, or of simple injury from passing vehicles. At the present day and in this country the danger last mentioned is the only one really to be feared, and it is so considerable that the question is often raised whether a lady be not safer at the right of her cavalier; but the still greater danger in this case of her being crushed between the horses, in case of either one springing suddenly towards the other, has caused it thus far to be decided in the negative.

There is also always a possibility—slight, doubtless—of a lady's getting kicked or bitten when on the right; and it might be difficult for her companion, without risk to her limbs, to seize her horse by the head should he become refractory. In case of its becoming absolutely necessary to take a terrified or exhausted rider off of an unmanageable horse, there would probably be time for her escort to cross behind her and place himself at her left hand.

Now that we are on the subject, we may give a word of caution as to some other dangers of the road. Among those to the rider, the most common is *shying;* but vigilance — and perpetual vigilance will be necessary—will reduce this to the rank of simple annoyance. Get your horse past the alarming object somehow, even if he has to be led; get him up to it if you can, and then pat and praise him; never let him hurry off after passing it; never whip him afterwards.

Rearing is less common than shying, but more dangerous from the risk of pulling the horse over backward. To rear he must, of course, spring up with the fore-legs, and if his intention can be divined in time it may perhaps be frustrated by a smart stroke down the shoulder; but an active animal is usually up before his rider has had time to think, and the question is how to come safe down again. To this end, on no account pull on the bit, but, without letting go the rein, grasp a thick lock of the mane and hold yourself with it as close to the neck as possible — which will throw your weight in the best place, and prepare you to leap down, should it be necessary. If you have kept perfectly calm, so that the horse has not suspected that you were frightened, he will doubtless come down on his feet, and very likely may not rear again. If, however, you feel his hind-legs sink under him, he will be intending to throw himself down, and you must jump down instantly to avoid getting caught under the saddle.

Kicking, when coming unexpectedly, is more likely than rearing to unseat the rider. If you withstand the first assault, however, get the horse's head up by an energetic use of the bit, and look out that he does not get it down again. It is needless to say that should either of the last two tricks become a habit, it will make the horse quite unfit for a lady's use.

If your horse is restless and disposed to jump, or perhaps run, when horses or vehicles rapidly approach him from behind, occupy his attention by moving the bit a little from side to side in his mouth.

Running away is undoubtedly serious business, but all authorities agree that the safest plan is to let the horse run, if there is room, and that the best lesson for him is to make him continue running after he wishes to stop. A steady pull on the bit is quite useless, and so is any cry of "Whoa! whoa!" at first. But after a little the bit should be vigorously *sawed*, so as to sway the head from side to side if possible, and thus confuse him, while you speak to him in a commanding tone.

The dangers to the horse upon the road, however, are greater and more numerous than to yourself, but they may almost all be averted by care and watchfulness on your part. Beware of a fast pace on hard macadam; beware of loose stones, which may bruise the frog or cause a tedious sprain; beware of food, water, above all, of currents of air when he is warm.

LESSON XV.

THE PIROUETTE, DEUX PISTES, PASSAGE.

IN the *pirouette ordinaire* of the French *manége* the horse turns upon one of his hind-legs, walking on the other three around it, just as in the *pirouette renversée*

ORDINARY PIROUETTE.

of Lesson XI. he turned upon one of the fore-legs, around which he walked upon the other three; and now, as then, the chief difficulty is to keep him from

GOING ON "DEUX PISTES."

moving the leg which is to serve as a pivot. The means for accomplishing this you have already ac-

THE PASSAGE.

quired, and a pressure of the heel on the one side, or of the crop on the other, will prevent an intended movement of the croup, while by the rein against the neck you move the forehand to the one side or to the other. In wheeling to the left it is the left hind-foot, and to the right the right hind-foot, which serves as a pivot. If your horse is stiff and clumsy in this exercise it will probably be because you have not got him together, with his hind-legs well under him, but at best you will probably find him less supple on one side than the other. Begin by moving the forehand but one step at a time, keeping your horse calm, so that he may not wound one foot with the other, holding your own person motionless, and gradually accustoming him to slight and delicate effects of hand, heel, and whip, so that he may to a by-stander appear to move of his own volition.

The *piste* (literally "trail" or "track") in the French *manége* is an imaginary circle lying three feet distant from the wall; which imaginary line, however, becomes in practice a well-defined path, which the horse soon learns to follow with little guidance from his rider. To go, then, "on two *pistes*" is to cause the horse to advance with his body placed obliquely, so that the hind-feet move on a different line from the fore-feet. In the cut the horse is shown directly across the *piste*.

The *passage* is a side movement without advancing. By it the cavalry close up their ranks, and to a civilian it is useful in many ways. Both of these movements you are now able to execute at pleasure.

LESSON XVI.

BACKING.

This lesson has been deferred thus far because, while it is one of the most practically and frequently useful, yet it is also the method which the horse naturally takes to escape from the unwonted constraint put upon the muscles of his neck and jaw in the course of the preceding lessons. You have had, therefore, to be on your guard hitherto against it; and had you taught it earlier you would have found your horse cunning enough to pretend to believe every play of the bit to be a signal to step back, and thus protract the instruction.

Having, then, got your horse, as usual, well in hand, lean back and give a pull on the reins. If he steps back, well; if not, touch him with the heel or tap his side with the crop, and when he lifts his foot to step forward repeat the pull on the reins, when the foot will be replaced farther back; then pat and praise him, and persevere until he will, at each tug of the reins, move backward one step and no more.

Should he swerve to right or left, straighten him by a tap or pressure of the crop on his right side, or by the

BACKING.

pressure of the heel on the left, as the case may require.

Your horse having learned to obey the pressure of the rein upon the neck, you may now, if you choose, adopt another method of holding the reins. It differs from that described in Lesson XIII. in that the two snaffle reins, instead of being separated by three fingers, have only one—the middle finger—between them; while the curb-reins, instead of coming into the hand between the snaffle-reins, come in below, having the little finger inserted between them.

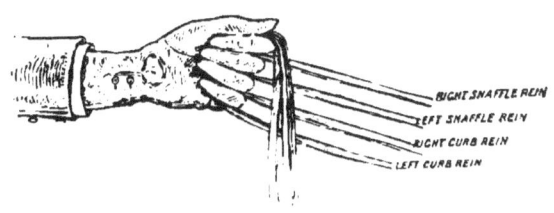

REINS IN HAND.

This method, though formerly the one usually taught, being that adopted by the English cavalry, has not, on

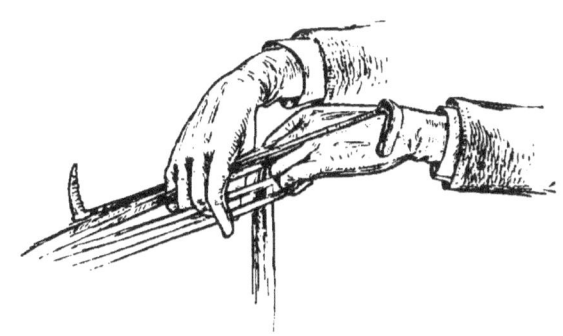

ACT OF CHANGING REINS.

the whole, as many advantages as the other for a civilian.

If you have occasion to use the left hand, or wish to

rest it, change the reins into the right hand by placing the right, still holding the whip, over and in front of the left, both palms downward, inserting the right forefinger between the reins separated by the left little finger, and so on, then grasping all together with the whip, and allowing the ends to pass out to the right.

This does not disarrange the reins, but makes it possible for you to take them back into the left hand in an instant by passing the left hand in like manner over the right.

LESSON XVII.

RIDING IN CIRCLES.—CHANGE OF LEADING FOOT.

You are now prepared to practise with profit a simple exercise, which you will find interesting to yourself, and, if carefully done, very improving to your horse. It is the riding in circles of small diameter. Mark out a number of rings of various sizes in some pasture-field with white pebbles or beans or small scraps of white paper, which may be scattered at intervals of two or three feet, so that the figures may not be remarked by the horse, but that he may receive his instruction from you only. Let the circles touch one another, so that you may change from one into the other, and thus turn to the right and left alternately. Begin at a walk, then proceed to a trot, practising first on the large circles, and then taking the smaller ones. Keep your horse "light in hand," and do not let him place his body across the line, but make him follow it accurately, with his neck and body bent around to the curve which it describes. When he is perfect in this exercise on level ground, move to some hill-side and begin again. When he can do figure 8's of a small size accurately at a smart

LEADING WITH THE RIGHT FORE-FOOT.

trot on a pretty steep slope, you may congratulate yourself on having made good progress, and may begin to do the large circles on level ground at a canter. Here comes in the troublesome matter of the " leading foot," and if you do not understand it, you must not be discouraged, for many persons ride "hit or miss" their whole lives long without thinking or knowing anything about it. The expression, besides, is misleading, and you will do well to study up the subject first on straight lines. Get a friend to canter beside you, and observe the motion of his horse's feet. You will see that the two fore-feet and the two hind-feet strike the ground not only one later than the other, but one in advance of the other, and that the one which leaves the ground last steps past the other and is planted farthest forward. It is this foot taking the long stride which is called, although it moves last, the " leading foot."

It ought not to make any difference to the horse with which foot he leads, nor to his rider, if a man, so long as he follows a straight line; but whenever he has to turn, it becomes both to horse and rider of importance—if the curve is sharp, of very great importance—that he should lead on the side towards which he is to turn.

A little observation of your companion's horse when turning will make the reason clear to you. A woman's seat being on the left side of the horse, it is easier for her that the shoulder having the most motion should be on the right side, and ladies' saddle-horses are consequently trained to lead with the right foot; the result,

LEADING WITH THE LEFT FORE-FOOT.

we may remark, often being that the fore-foot which does most work gives out before the others.

The horse so trained, however, is in this way always

ready to wheel to the right; but when he turns to the left, whether carrying man or woman, he must change and lead with the left foot; and if he has not sense enough to do so himself, you must teach him.

This, really, is not an easy task for an amateur, especially for the amateur feminine, who has not the efficient masculine resource of a pair of spurred heels. Even with their aid a man is often so embarrassed to make his horse comprehend that he gives up the attempt, and contents himself with "slowing down" before turning, his failure usually resulting from the insufficient previous training of the horse, coupled with his own ignorance of the successive short steps by which the latter may be led up to the performance of the wished-for act.

If you have been exact in the instruction hitherto given—if your bitting has been so thorough that your horse remains "light in hand" during all the manœuvres described in the foregoing lessons; if he responds instantly to the pressure of the rein upon the neck, and to the touch of the heel and of the whip upon the flank, so that you can move the forehand and the croup separately or at the same time in the same or in opposite directions; if he will rise from a walk into a canter without trotting; and if, finally, your drilling in the flexions of the neck permits you to bend his head to right or left when at rest or in motion without affecting the position of the forehand—then your horse is thoroughly prepared for the present lesson ; and the same tact and patience which have brought you on thus far will assuredly carry you triumphantly through it.

First, however, you should learn to tell with which foot you are leading, and you can do so by leaning forward in the saddle while cantering, when you will see that the knee of the leading leg is thrown up higher than its fellow, and by bending still farther you may see this foot planted in advance upon the ground. If your horse has never been trained, it is as likely to be one foot as the other. Now, the first step to be taken is to put your horse in such a position that it will be easy and natural for him to lead off with the desired foot, and awkward to lead off with the other. This position is with the head turned in the direction you wish to go, and with the croup advanced a little in the same direction, so that the body is placed obliquely across the line of advance. Thus, if you wish to lead with the right foot, you keep his head turned in the direction you wish to go, while with the heel you move the croup over two steps to the right; then, touching him with the heel and raising the hand, you give the signal to canter, and he will probably lead off with the right foot. If not, stop him and try again, giving him a sharp cut with your whip just behind the right shoulder.. To lead with the left the process is reversed, the croup being moved two steps to the left before the signal to canter is given, a sudden dig with the heel behind the shoulder conveying to the horse the hint to hurry forward his left leg. You can now begin to canter on the circles you have marked out; you will, however, at first come down to a walk before changing from one circle to an adjoining one—which change, of course, reverses the curve, and makes it necessary to change the leading foot.

This figure eight riding, thus, ∞, is most useful both for horse and rider when it is carefully done. Keep the horse "light in hand," and above all, *collected—viz.*, with his haunches well under him, and always with his feet exactly in the circle and his neck and body bent to the curve. As soon as he will lead off correctly from a walk, begin to teach him to do so from the trot; and when this lesson has been learned, practise him on the double circles, or figure 8's, beginning at a trot, and lifting him into a canter just as you pass from one circle to the other. This will accustom him to the idea of a change of movement at the time of a change in direction. Having got him to canter, continue on the same circle many times around and around, then bring him to a trot, and pass to the adjoining circle, lifting him to a canter just as you turn into it, as before, but of course leading with the opposite foot. Make your circles smaller and smaller, and continue till he has had time to appreciate the importance of leading correctly; then try to make him change at a canter, choosing for the purpose one of your smallest figure 8's, and indicating to him the change of foot on the same spot and in the same way as when you began by trotting, and you will no doubt be immediately successful.

If the horse in changing the lead of the fore-feet does not make the corresponding change with the hind-feet, he is said to be *disunited*. This fault must be corrected immediately, as it renders his gait not only uncomfortable to the rider, but very insecure.

PART II.
ETIQUETTE IN THE SADDLE.

There is a large class of excellent people who feel a decided impatience at the very name of etiquette. "It is all nonsense," they say, and they will give you various infallible receipts for getting on without such an objectionable article. One admonishes you to be "natural," and your manners will leave nothing to be desired. Another sagaciously defines politeness to be "kindness kindly expressed," and intimates that if your heart is right your deportment cannot fail to be so too. All these philosophizings, however, give little comfort to the bashful young person just venturing into society, for unfortunately few of us are so happily constituted as always to think, much less to say and do, exactly the right thing at the right time, and the most unobservant presently discovers, very likely at the cost of no small mortification, that the usages of society, even when apparently arbitrary, cannot be disregarded with impunity. In the etiquette of the saddle, however, common-sense takes so decidedly precedence of the arbitrary and conventional that no courageous, kind-hearted, and sensible young girl, however inexperienced, need be afraid of committing any fatal solecism. The reason of this is that the element of danger is never entirely absent, and that the importance of assuring the safety and comfort of yourself and companions, to say nothing of lookers-on and passers-by, or of the noble and valuable animal you ride, far transcends that of observing any mere forms and ceremonies.

DRESS.

Fashion at present, both in this country and in England, requires that the whole riding costume be as simple as possible, and entirely without ornament. Formerly much more latitude was allowed, and very pretty effects were produced with braid trimming across the breast, a little color at the neck, and a slouched hat with long feather or floating veil—witness the picture of the Empress Eugénie when Countess Montijo, and many a charming family portrait besides—but now fashion pronounces all that sort of thing "bad form," and a word to the wise is sufficient. The habit itself must be quite dark, or even black, perfectly plain in the waist, with black buttons up to the neck, and with a scant, short skirt only just long enough to cover the feet. The cuffs and collar must be of plain linen, no color or flutter of ribbon being anywhere permissible. The handkerchief must not be thrust in the breast, but kept in

ETIQUETTE IN THE SADDLE.

the saddle pocket, and if a veil is worn, it must be short and black. The hair should be so securely put up that it will not shake down, and that the hair-pins will not work out. In the matter of the hat more freedom of choice is allowed, and in the country almost anything may be worn, but wherever there is any pretence of dressing, the only correct thing is the regulation silk "cylinder," which, by-the-bye, usually looks better rather low in the crown, and which is every way a pleasanter and more serviceable hat than ladies who have never worn one are apt to imagine. About the cutting of a riding-habit, it may be remarked, there is nothing mysterious, although one might think so from the way it is often talked about, especially in the advertisements of fashionable tailors, and there is no reason in the world why any clever young girl should not make one for herself if she chooses. The only eccentricity about it, from the dress-making point of view, is the shaping out of a place for the right knee, so that the skirt may hang straight and not ruck up, and this can easily be managed at home by improvising a horse with a couple of chairs and a rolled-up rug, putting the saddle on it, and trying the effect in place. Be careful to leave plenty of room across the breast. A couple of straps should be sewn inside in the proper place, so that the toe or heel of each foot may be inserted to prevent the skirt from rising and exposing the feet; and these straps should not be strong, but, on the contrary, like all other parts of the skirt, and particularly the facing, should be made so as certainly to tear loose instantly in case of getting caught in a fall. Before leaving the habit, we may remark that the wearer should practise gathering it up, holding it in one hand, and walking in it at home, and if possible before a mirror. No petticoats ought to be worn, but merino drawers, and easy trousers of the same stuff as the rest of the habit. Beware of badly made seams, which have a vexatious way, as many a masculine wearer can testify, of pinching out a bit of skin at some inopportune moment. The trousers should be cut away a little over the instep, and fastened down under the sole with straps, which may be either sewed on or attached by buttons inside the band, in which case india-rubber is the best material, being easy alike on buttons, stuff, and fingers. Corsets should be worn as usual, but never laced tight, and it would be better that they should not have steel clasps or steel springs, which might be dangerous in case of a fall. The boots should be easy, broad-soled, low-heeled, and rather laced than buttoned, as less likely on the one hand to catch in the stirrup, and on the other to bruise the foot by chafing against the saddle. The gloves should be strong, but supple and easy, as it is important that every finger should have free and independent movement. Tight gloves not only benumb the hands in cold weather, but always cause an awkward handling of the reins, and may be positively dangerous with a fresh horse. As to the relative merits of crop and whip, there is room for difference of opinion. By many persons the former is looked upon as a senseless affectation of English ways, but the fact is that with a horse regularly trained to the saddle it is more useful than a whip, as by its aid a lady can "collect" her horse—that is, can make him bring his hind-legs under him, in the same way that a man does by the pressure of his calves. If, however, the horse has never been trained, and is sluggish or wilful, a whip may be more useful. Whichever of the two produces the better results will have the more "workmanlike" look and be in the "better form."

THE MOUNT.

It is undoubtedly much pleasanter and more exhilarating to ride a good and handsome horse than a poor and ugly one, a horse adapted to one's size and weight than one too large or too small, too heavy or too light; but none of these points are matters of etiquette. On this whole subject etiquette makes only one demand, but that one is inexorable — it is *perfect neatness*. A lady's mount must be immaculate from ear to hoof, in coat and mane and entire equipment. It is in a great degree their exquisite neatness that gives such an air of style not only to English horsewomen, but to English turn-outs of all kinds, which, nevertheless, have not usually the "spick and span new" look of fashionable American equipages. On coming out, therefore, prepared for a ride, take time to look your horse over swiftly, but keenly, noting first that his eye and general appearance indicate good health and spirits; secondly, that he has been thoroughly groomed, his mane freed from dandruff, his hoofs washed, but not blacked; thirdly, that the saddle and bridle are perfectly clean and properly put on. Every buckle should have been undone and cleansed, the leather suppled, and the bright metal polished; the girths, three in number — never fewer than two — should be snug, but not tight enough to impede free breathing; the bits in their proper place, that is to say, the snaffle just high enough up not to wrinkle the corners of the mouth, and the curb considerably lower, with its chain, which should pass below the snaffle, lying flat and smooth against the skin in the chin groove; finally, the throat-latch loose. While it is not always wise to reprimand carelessness on the part of your groom on the spot, it is well never to let it pass unnoticed, while, on the other hand, it is a good plan always to show appreciation of especial attention to your wishes by a kind word or a smile.

MOUNTING.

It is rather a trying ordeal for an inexperienced rider to mount a tall horse from the ground, even when there are no lookers-on, and many a one remains in bondage to chairs and horse-blocks all her life long rather than undertake it. The feat, however, is really so much ea-

ETIQUETTE IN THE SADDLE.

sier than it looks, and when well performed makes the rider appear so agile and graceful, giving such an air of style and *savoir-faire* to the departure, that it is well worth every lady's while to acquire it. The first requisite is that the horse should stand still, and for this purpose the attendant should have given him some preliminary exercise, as the fresh air and bright light are so exhilarating to a high-strung horse that he cannot at first restrain his impulse to caper about. This preparatory airing should be entered upon invariably as calmly as possible, and begun at a walk, for a flurry at starting, and especially the use of the whip, will often disturb a horse's nerves for hours, making him unpleasant if not dangerous to ride. When the horse is brought to the door, let the groom stand directly in front of him, holding the bridle not by the rein, but with both hands by each cheek, just above the bit. If he is a proud and sensitive animal, do not rush up to him excitedly with a slamming of doors and gates, nor allow any one else to do so, but approach with gentle steadiness. Stand a moment and look him over, give your orders quietly, and pat his neck for a moment, speaking pleasantly to him the while, so that he may get accustomed to your voice.

Now standing with your right side a few inches from the saddle, facing the same way as the horse, and with your left shoulder slightly thrown back, place the right hand on the second pommel, holding in it the whip, and the reins drawn just tight enough to give a feeling of the bit. Your attendant will stand facing you, and as close as convenient, and will now stoop forward, with his hands clasped and with his right forearm firmly supported on his right thigh. Now with your left hand lift your riding-skirt in front, and place your left foot

READY TO MOUNT.

in his hands. Let go the skirt, rest your left hand on his shoulder, and giving him the cue by bending the right knee, spring up erect on the left foot, and, seating yourself sideways on the saddle, place the right knee over the horn.

If your attendant is unused to rendering such service, you had better make your first essays in some secluded place, in which you can instruct him where to stand, just how high to lift your foot, and caution him to put forth strength enough to support you steadily, without

"ONE, TWO, THREE."

lifting too violently. Do not be deterred by awkwardness on his part or on your own from learning to mount from the ground, for the more awkward, the better practice for you. Your attendant will now lift your skirt above the knee, so that it will hang properly without dragging, and then disengaging the stirrup from beneath the skirt, will place your left foot in it.

PLACING THE FOOT IN THE STIRRUP.

Too much care cannot be taken with the position in the saddle, which should be exactly as shown in the following cut. The left leg should invariably hang perpendicularly from the knee, with the heel depressed, and with the foot parallel with the horse's side. The length of the stirrup-strap should be such that the knee thus is out of contact with the hunting-horn, but near enough to be brought firmly up against it by raising the heel. The right knee should rest easily but snugly over the pommel, so as to grasp it in case the horse springs. Neither foot should be allowed to sway about nor to project so as to be seen awkwardly poking out the skirt.

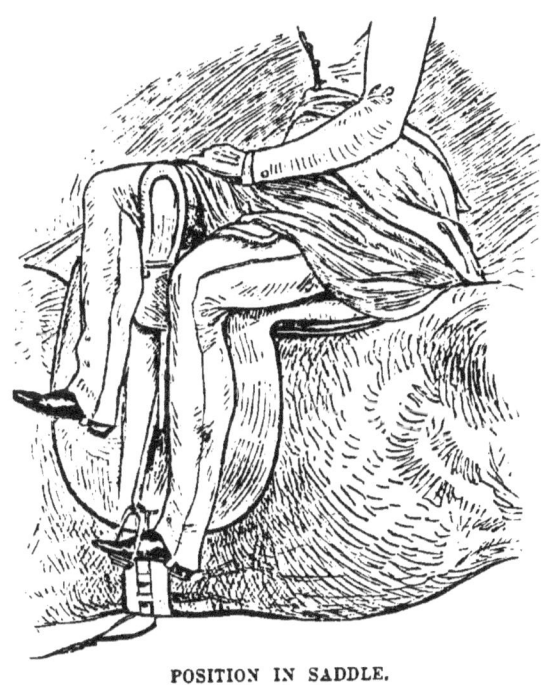

POSITION IN SADDLE.

If your clothing does not feel quite comfortable, rise in your stirrup and shake it down, resting your hand, if necessary, on your attendant's shoulder, for it will be very awkward should it become disarranged on the road. Now put your handkerchief in the saddle pocket, take the reins in the left hand, or in both hands, as you prefer, and start the horse by a touch with the heel.

It is, of course, the correct thing to mount from the ground, if possible, but here again common-sense comes so decidedly to the front that it is not too much to say that the sole indispensable requirement of an enlightened etiquette is *good-nature*. Certain it is that the eye masculine will follow with pleasure, and perhaps with some emotion, the movements of the young girl who comes out bright and fresh, gives her horse a pat or two, with a lump of sugar, as she glances him quickly over, looks kindly at her stable-boy, and then skips gayly into the saddle from a chair brought out by a maid, while the same eye will rest quite unmoved, except by a spirit of criticism, on the self-conscious and selfish damsel, though she be put on in the most approved manner by the smartest groom who ever wore top-boots. Mount, then, from the ground, if you have some one to put you on and some one to hold your horse; or, if the horse will stand without holding, cautioning your escort—if you are not sure of his expertness in such services—to be sure to raise your foot straight up, and to give you warning by counting one, two, so that you may be certain to have the leg straightened before he begins to lift, as otherwise the result may be the reverse of graceful. When in the saddle, rise in your stirrup, as already suggested, and smooth down your dress, meantime thanking your escort and telling him how well he did it. This smoothing down of the skirt it is a good plan to practise frequently, first standing, then at a walk, then at a trot, till you can do it deftly, almost without thought, for there is no telling at what inopportune moment it may become necessary.

To mount from the ground without assistance is a feat which few ladies would voluntarily undertake. It may be accomplished in an emergency, however, if the horse is quiet and not too tall, by lowering the stirrup sufficiently to reach it with the left foot, and springing up with the aid of the hands, the left of which should grasp the mane and the right the cantle of the saddle.

THE START.

Do not put your horse in motion by a cut with the whip, which would be trying to his nerves, nor by chirping or clucking, which would be equally trying to the nerves of your companions, but by a touch with the heel, or a pressure between your heel on the left side and your crop on the right. If other ladies are to be mounted, move on so far that they will be in no danger, either real or imaginary, from your horse's heels, and never at any time put him in such a position that he can kick any one, or that you can get kicked yourself by any other horse. If you have to turn about on starting, try to do so by making your horse step around with his hind-legs (in the technical phrase, *pirouette renversée*), so as to avoid turning your back and presenting his haunches towards any one with whom you may be talking or from whom you are to take leave. To be able to do this easily and gracefully you must have him well "collected" and "light in hand."

ON WHICH SIDE TO RIDE.

The next question that arises is on which side of her escort a lady should ride. This point, so much discussed and disputed in this country, is scarcely raised in England, where the universal habit of turning to the left makes it, under almost all circumstances, safer for her to be on his left, in which position he finds himself always interposed between his charge and any passing vehicle, whether it come from before or from behind. In this country, however, we have adopted — nobody knows why, unless it is because the French do so — the rule of keeping to the right, and yet without changing our manner of riding and driving, so that the result is often awkward and even dangerous. The teamster who used to walk on the left of his horses, so as to lead them out of the way when occasion required, still walks on the left, which now puts him in the middle of the road; the coachman still sits on the right, though the probability of contact has changed over to the other side; the lady's seat is still on the left side of the horse, which obliges her to choose between the danger of being caught by passing wheels or crushed by the horse of her escort. As there is no reason in the world, whether in the conformation of the female form or of the horse itself, or in the exigencies of equestrianism, that makes it inherently more proper to sit on one side of the horse rather than on the other, it seems strange that none of our independent American ladies should have undertaken to set the fashion of sitting on the right side. The Princess of Wales always does so, for some special reason. The Empress of Austria, who is well known as one of the boldest and most graceful riders as well as one of the most beautiful women in Europe, is said to have saddles made in both ways, using them alternately, and this plan is adopted by more than one of the noble ladies of England who hunt regularly in the season, with a view of preventing too constant a strain on the same set of nerves, and possibly causing an unequal development of the two sides of the person. However, accepting the present feminine seat as a thing not to be changed, the advantages in this country of riding on the one hand of the escort or on the other are so equally divided that the balance may incline to either side, and a lady is always free to do about it as she pleases without exciting remark. When riding on the right side, the lady is protected from passing vehicles, and the gentleman has his right hand free to assist her in any way, even to taking her off her horse in case of necessity; but if either horse were to shy towards the other, she might get bruised, and she is always liable to an occasional contact with her companion's person, which may not be pleasant. Children should certainly be kept on the right, and so should any inexperienced or very timid person; and at all times a gentleman should interpose himself between the lady under his charge and danger of any kind — as, for instance, reckless drivers, rude strollers, or a drove of cattle. When riding on the left, the lady is undoubtedly in a more exposed position, especially if her horse is disposed to dance or shy at rattling wagons and the like; but her escort, being able to ride closer to her, is enabled more quickly and safely to take the animal by the head, if necessary, and under all circumstances he should hold his reins and whip in his right hand, and in case of danger keep his horse well "collected," so as to be ready to act promptly and without any show of excitement.

THE SEAT.

Position.—The lady's position on horseback is so conspicuous that the fact ought to stimulate the most indifferent so to place and carry herself as to show her figure to the best advantage, and this graceful carriage of the person will be found to be the first step towards achieving a firm and easy seat. The posture should be erect, the back slightly hollowed, the breast thrown forward, the chin drawn in so that the neck will be nearly vertical. The lower limbs should rest easily but firmly in their respective places, the left leg hanging perpendicularly from the knee downward, with heel slightly depressed, and foot parallel with the horse's side, the right toe raised a little above the horizontal, but not carried far enough forward to poke up the riding habit. The seat should be in the middle of the saddle, not on the right side of it with the body inclined to the left, which is excessively awkward, nor on the left side with an inclination to the right, which is equally awkward, and with the additional disadvantage of being sure to cause saddle galls. When the body is consciously *balanced* on the horse's back, when the shoulders are equidistant from his ears, and when the eyes, looking be-

A SQUARE AND PROPER SEAT.

tween said ears (an excellent habit), look straight along the road, and not off obliquely to one side of it, then the seat, whatever else it may not be, is at least in the middle of the saddle.

The Hand.—As to the manner of carrying the arms, Colonel Hayes remarks that he has seen of late (in England) some ladies sticking out their elbows, but that he, for his part, decidedly approves of the old rule which forbade that daylight should be seen between a lady's arms and body. The sight which annoyed Colonel Hayes is not unknown in America, but probably most observers correctly attribute it either to ignorance or affectation. Certainly there is no reason for it, whether practical or æsthetic, as the raising of the elbows lifts the hands into a position in which the reins act less correctly on the horse's mouth, while substituting angles for curves in the outline of the figure, and quite destroying the air of well-bred repose which is one of the great charms of a finished horsewoman. The arms should hang naturally by the sides, with the hands, a few inches apart, just above the knee, and as low as possible without resting on it, the nails turned down, the knuckles at an angle of forty-five degrees with the horizon, the wrists bent inward so as to permit of a little play of the wrist joint at each tug of the horse on the reins.

The Poise.—All this is not very difficult so long as the horse keeps quiet, or even when he merely walks; but how is this much-admired statuesque repose to be preserved at the trot, the canter, the gallop, to say nothing of incidental shying and capering? There is only one answer to this question, and that is—*practice*. But even practice is usually not sufficient without an accompaniment, infrequent and not always pleasant, *viz.*, frank and unflattering criticism; and every one who really wishes to excel, and to merit the praises which as woman she is certain to receive, will see to it that this wholesome corrective is often at hand. Practice itself, to be profitable, must be intelligent, and the cause of any discomfort from the motion of the horse should be sought out and removed. It will be found almost always to result from involuntary muscular contractions, especially of the waist, which should invariably be kept supple, as it is to a slight play of loin and thigh that the rider must look to prevent being thrown up by each spring of the hind-legs in cantering or galloping.

In rising to the trot, bear outwardly with the left heel, which will keep the knee close against the saddle, and prevent the leg from swaying about. At the same time be careful not to rise towards the left—an awkward but very common habit, which can be detected by the plan already suggested of sighting between the horse's ears. Mr. Sidney says, "The ideal of a fine horsewoman is to be erect without being rigid, square to the front, and until quite at home in the saddle, looking religiously between her horse's ears. The shoulders must therefore be square, but thrown back a little, so as to expand the chest and make a hollow waist, such as is observed in waltzing, but always flexible. On the flexibility of the person above the waist, and on the firmness below, all the grace of equestrianism, all the safety, depend. Nervousness makes both men and women poke their heads forward—a stupid trick in a man, unpardonable in a woman. A lady should bend like a willow in a storm, always returning to an easy and nearly upright position. Nothing but practice—frequent, but not too long continued—can establish the all-important balance. Practice, and practice only, enables the rider instinctively to bear to the proper side, or lean back, as a horse turns, bounds, or leaps." It is evidently not simply pounding along the high-road in a straight line on a steady nag which is here meant. The following advice, given by a lady who is herself an accomplished horsewoman, will furnish a clew to the sort of exercise which will be really profitable. She says, "Let the pupil practise riding in circles to the right, sitting upright, but bending a little to the horse's motion, following his nose with her eye; beginning with a walk, proceed to a slow trot, increasing the action as she gains firmness in the saddle. When in a smart trot on a circle to the right she can, leaning as she should to the right, see the feet of the horse on the right side, it may be assumed that she has arrived at a firm seat." Another excellent exercise is to lean over, now to one side, now to the other, now in front, far enough to observe the horse's action, the motion of his feet, and the regularity of his step.

ON THE ROAD.

If good-nature is the quality most essential to *mounting* in a pleasing manner, that which will cause a lady to shine most *on the road* is kindness. Such a statement will perhaps bring a smile to the lips of some dashing girl who thinks that she has other means of pleasing, once mounted on a spirited horse, than the practice of any of the Christian virtues; but the writer, after many years' experience with *amazones* both young and old, believes it to be literally true. A lady who, without weakness, is gentle and thoughtful, will have, other things being equal, more sympathetic obedience from her horse, a finer hand, a more supple seat, and will bring him back fresher and her whole party home in better spirits than one who is not. To begin with, there is almost always one of the horses which is not equal to the others, but keeps up with difficulty, and as it is precisely that horse which should set the pace for the rest, it is well to observe the capacity of the different animals, and spare the feelings of any one of the party who may be poorly mounted. One might hardly suppose it necessary to mention so elementary a rule of politeness as that which bids us, when we ride in company, not to keep always in the best part of the road; but horses are sometimes selfish as well as human beings, and the selfish horse, like the selfish man, unless he is prevented, will imperceptibly crowd his patient companion into the ruts, when the rider will get the credit or discredit of the action. Another too common piece of thoughtlessness is the splashing at full speed through mud puddles, the result of which is naturally more apparent to one's neighbors than to one's self. If to an equestrian, however, being splashed or spattered is annoying, to a pedestrian it is nothing less than exasperating, and such a one will look after the person guilty of the rudeness with eyes of anything but admiration. One cannot be too careful, indeed, when riding near pedestrians, as they are decidedly susceptible under such circumstances, and likely to take offence; and especially is caution required where women and children are concerned, for it is impossible to conjecture what they will do if suddenly startled by the rapid approach of horses. The writer saw, one afternoon, a nursery-maid crossing Rotten Row with a baby-carriage (*Anglice, perambulator*), and two children holding to her skirts. When half-way over, a lady and three gentlemen came galloping down, followed by two grooms. The children scattered, the riders could not pull up, and for an instant it seemed as if the little party were doomed to destruction, as the horses appeared to pass right over some of them. The English rule, not only for country riding, but for the Park or other public places (and an excellent one it is), requires a gentleman to pull up and pass a lady, if alone, at a walk, whether she be on foot or on horseback, and though more latitude may be allowed a lady, yet she should not gallop up suddenly behind another lady who is alone, as a nervous horse might be so excited as to cause great uneasiness to a timid rider. If you should unfortunately produce such a result, by all means pause and express regret, and if your horse is quiet, offer to ride for a few minutes beside the sufferer—for so she may be called. In passing on the road, the rule is, when meeting, to keep to the right, but when overtaking, to pass to the left, and in like manner, when overtaken, to keep to the right, so as to leave the road free at your left. The only exception to this rule is in the case of led-horses, which, as they are often inclined to kick, should be avoided by passing next to the one ridden. When approaching a lady in a public place a gentleman should always do so on the off or right side.

It is sometimes rather a nice point to decide when assistance ought to be offered by a gentleman to a lady with whom he is not acquainted, and, if offered, whether it ought to be accepted. The following incident, recounted by Sir Joseph Arnould in his "Life of Lord Chief-justice Denman," is interesting as showing how such a question was discussed in what may certainly be considered as among the very best society in England. He says that on occasion of a visit which the Lord Chief-justice paid to Walmer Castle, three years before the

Duke of Wellington's death, in a conversation about riding, the duke said, "When I meet a lady on horseback I always stop, and if her horse seems troublesome, offer to ride alongside her in the Row till it is quiet. The other day I met a lady on a fresh, violent horse, so I took off my hat and said, 'Shall I ride with you? My horse is perfectly quiet.' She knew me, for she replied, 'No, your Grace; I think I can get on very well.' After she was gone, I felt sure it was Jenny Lind." "We all agreed," adds Lord Denman, "that the great singer should have accepted the services of the great duke, whether she wanted them or not."

It is better not to fight a restive horse unless you have reason to be sure of victory, but rather get some one to lead him past the object or into the road which he may have taken it into his foolish head to object to. If he is in "that state of nervous irritability known as *freshness*," do not jerk the bit, but keep a steady, patient bearing on it, speaking soothingly to him in a low though steady voice, for his acute hearing will enable him to perceive distinctly tones which are almost or quite inaudible to your companions. Try not to have an anxious expression of countenance, no matter what he may do, but to look serene and smiling, as it will not only be more becoming, but will undoubtedly react upon your own feelings. If he pulls, it is well to take the slack of the right reins in the spare fingers of the left, and *vice versa*, as this will give a firmer hold, and enable you to shorten the reins without relaxing their tension.

Always speak to your horse on approaching and on leaving him, and also whenever he has tried especially

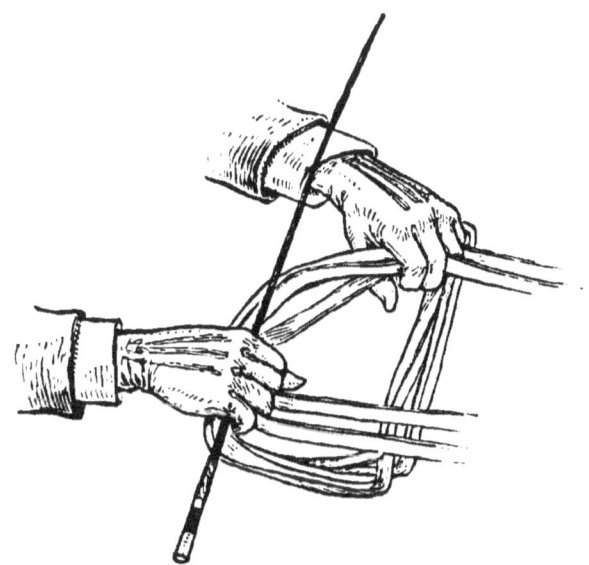

METHOD OF HOLDING THE REINS IN BOTH HANDS.

to please you, as your voice will soon come to have a great influence over him. There is a story told of two keepers in a zoological garden, one of whom was a favorite with the animals, while the other, though a more conscientious man, was disliked by them. The authorities, curious to learn the reason, had them watched, and it was found that the former always talked to the animals, while the latter served them silently. Too much conversation with one's horse, however, is apt to get to be a bore to one's companions.

THE PACE.

This should vary with the nature of the ground, as it is dangerous to the horse, and consequently very bad form, to ride fast on a very rough or hard road. If slippery, a smart trot is safer than a slow trot or walk; but if walking, by all means let the horse have his head. If a steep place is to be descended, attack it at right angles, and not obliquely, for, when going down straight, a slip is likely to have no worse result than a momentary sitting down on the haunches, whereas, if going diagonally, it would probably bring the horse down flat. The canter, which is peculiarly the lady's pace, is much harder than the trot on the horse's feet and legs, especially on the leading foot and leg, and it should be reserved for comparatively soft ground. The lead with the right foot is easier for a lady, owing to her one-sided seat, than that with the left, and it would be considered awkward or ignorant for her not to start off with the right, although during a long ride it is well to change, so as to bring the strain upon a new set of muscles.

TURNING.

Of course in turning you must always lead towards the turn, that is, with the right foot in turning to the right, and with the left in turning to the left. For instance, if you have to round a corner to the right, and are leading with the right foot, as will probably be the case, you have nothing to do but to go on around, being careful to choose good footing for your horse, and avoiding particularly loose stones. If, however, you are leading with the left, you must change, and you can best do so in the following manner. As you approach the critical spot, *collect* your horse with the curb, and bring him to a trot; then, just as you reach the corner, make him swerve slightly to the left and instantly give the signal to canter, at the same time turning him sharply to the right, pressing your heel against his side back of the girth, and lifting the right snaffle-rein. It is well to draw back the right shoulder also, so as to throw your weight on his left side, and leave his right leg free to make the long stride. As this is by no means an easy operation for an unskilled rider, except on a perfectly trained horse, I will give the directions also in detail for the reverse process of wheeling to the left. If your horse should be leading with the left foot, you have, of course, no change to make. If, however, you are, as usual, leading with the right, you must "change the leg" to the left. As you draw near the corner, moderate your speed and collect your horse with the curb, bringing him to a trot. Then, just at the moment of turning, sway his shoulders a very little to the right, give the signal to canter by raising your hand, and wheel sharply to the left, at the same time pressing your crop against his right side back of the girth, and raising the left snaffle-rein. While doing so, draw back your left shoulder so as to throw your weight on the right side. If he does not take the hint at once, do not be discouraged, but practise him in some quiet place, choosing, if possible, a corner where the turn is uphill; and when he does well, pat him and make much of him, for you will find that no one of your admirers is more sensitive to your praises than he. This matter of turning is well worth all the trouble it may cost you, as it will give you a lively pleasure to find your horse's powerful limbs moving sympathetically to the gentle impulses of a woman's hand, and, besides, it lends an air of style and *savoir-faire* which will be fully appreciated by every looker-on who knows anything whatever about riding. Be particular to lean over towards the centre of the curve you are describing at an angle proportionate to the speed, just as the horse does himself, that is, leaning to the right side as he wheels to the right, and to the left when he wheels to the left. It is well not to let him cut off his corners, but to preserve the same distance from the centre of the road, just as if you were riding in company, and when this last is the case be careful to keep exactly abreast both on the straight road and on the turns, for there is nothing that looks more countrified than to see riders straggling along irregularly like a party of mechanics out for a stroll on a Sunday afternoon.

ETIQUETTE IN THE SADDLE.

It is well never to canter a carriage-horse unless you know him well, and are sure he will not thus be rendered unsteady in harness, and in like manner you should be considerate of your escort or companions, and not urge their horses beyond their proper gait. A good way to do, if you are much the best mounted of the party, is now and then, when the road is suitable, to gallop on and return again. It looks well to see a lady cantering beside a gentleman who is trotting; but the reverse never seems quite good form, and especially when it is evident that the gentleman's horse is galloping because he has been pushed off his legs.

A borrowed horse is an article which is looked upon with very different eyes by the elderly people who generally are the lenders, and the youthful riders that are usually the borrowers, and many a man, and perhaps many a woman too, remembers with shame and regret how little were appreciated or deserved the favors of this sort received in youthful days. A borrowed horse should be scrupulously ridden exactly as the owner wishes, and moreover the owner's desires ought to be respectfully ascertained in advance.

For cross-country riding the stirrups should be taken up at least one hole, and the same is advisable in mounting a strange horse. Another safe precaution, in the latter case, is a running martingale, which will prevent him from throwing up his head, as some horses have the habit of doing, to the great annoyance of the rider.

There are two or three more practical suggestions which may not be out of place here. The first and most important is that it is exceedingly dangerous to let a horse stand in a draught of air, or in a cool place, or eat or drink, when heated. In ten minutes he may be so crippled that he will never take a free step again. Ferry-boats are notoriously bad places, and a horse should never be taken on to them till quite cool. It is not well to let your horse crop the leaves or grass, as kind-hearted riders permit him to do sometimes, for it soils his lips and bits, giving him a slovenly air, and you run the risk besides of his wiping them on your habit before you part from him. Avoid letting your horse drink unless he really would be better for the refreshment, as he can hardly do so without wetting the curb-reins, making them stiff and dirty-looking.

THE GROOM.

The costume of the groom is too well known to require remark further than that it should be scrupulously neat. In the country, top-boots, etc., are by no means *de rigueur*, and under many circumstances would savor more of pretence than of real gentility. The groom ought to be mounted on a strong and able horse, which, if unused to the saddle, he should train at least so far that he can with one hand, by the aid of his legs, force it to take and keep any position. When accompanying inexperienced riders his horse should be able to overtake theirs easily. The distance at which he should ride behind his mistress varies with circumstances—in a crowded street his place being close behind her, while in the Park or in the country he naturally falls farther back, though never beyond easy call. If he is mounted on a good saddle-horse, he should keep in his place, that is, always at the same distance, galloping if necessary; but if riding a carriage-horse, as is often convenient, he should not, unless absolutely necessary, force the animal beyond the fastest trot at which it looks well in harness. He should never canter any horse unless instructed expressly to do so, but should trot in a business-like way, rising in his stirrups, or, if necessary, should gallop, sitting straight, with hands low and feet thrust home in the stirrups. In all cases he should look straight forward, without appearing to notice what goes on around him. Nothing looks in worse form than a groom sitting lazily back on a cantering horse, and casting glances at the admiring nursery-maids along the way. When summoned to his mistress, he should touch his hat to acknowledge receipt of the command, and should ride quickly up on the off side, where he should listen in a respectful attitude with eyes cast down, then, touching his hat again, depart to carry out her orders.

PART III.

LEAPING

ONE pleasant winter afternoon a fashionably dressed young man, crop in hand, spur on heel, and mounted on a tall horse, was seen to emerge briskly from a little grove in a gentleman's place, and come to a sudden halt in the level field across which he had intended to gallop. The cause was a new ditch, deep though narrow, stretching across from fence to fence before him. He looked at the obstacle a moment, then up and down the field, and remarked to a gardener, an old Scotchman, who stood looking on, spade in hand, "Well, I suppose I must go back." "I suppose so," said the old fellow, dryly, looking up out of the corner of his eye with an almost imperceptible smile. The young man reddened, hesitated, and then turned away, saying, as if the other's thoughts had been spoken out, "To tell the truth, I don't know whether my horse would if he could, nor whether he could if he would." "An' the same o' yourself," muttered the old man in his grizzled beard. The sarcasm was not to be wondered at, as the speaker remembered what he had many a time seen, and very likely himself done in his younger days in some hunting field of the old country, for the ditch before him could have been cleared by an active boy, on his own legs, with a good run. Moreover, it is not improbable that the reader is ready to agree with the old satirist in thinking the young man a "muff." Nevertheless, both

APPROACHING A FENCE.

horse and rider might easily have come to grief, for the steep banks were crumbly, and while the rider's seat was not of the firmest, his mount was straight in the shoulder and a little stiff in the pastern. However, they were both as well fitted to overcome such a difficulty as nine-tenths of American horses and riders, and a very little previous practice would have enabled them to spring over without bestowing a second thought upon it. The total indifference on this subject of leaping among our people is really quite remarkable, for one can hardly take a ride anywhere in the country without there arising some occasions when even a little knowledge of the art would have added to one's pleasure. How often, for instance, an easy fence separates the dusty road, too hard as well as too hot for fast riding, from some cool wood with its shaded turf, where a gallop would be delightful and would do the horse good instead of harm. The reason of this indifference is not only the fear of getting shaken off, but a doubt as to the horse's ability to leap, and a dread of doing him some harm by such an unusual exertion. All these apprehensions are very likely well-founded, for if you have never done any leaping your first essay will, in all probability, give you a severe shock. Then if your horse is green at this sort of work, and the fence is at all difficult, he will not improbably refuse altogether, or jump so unwillingly and clumsily as to risk your bones as well as his own; and if he does not really fall, he may cause such a strain upon unaccustomed muscles as to set up a "splint" or "spavin," producing at least temporary lameness. Nevertheless, all these excellent reasons for not trying to leap can gradually, but rapidly and with perfect safety, be removed by practice, and practice of a kind very pleasant and interesting, while at the same time improving to your seat, giving it a firmness under all circumstances which no amount of riding on the highway could ever do.

Some horses are exceedingly fond of leaping, but the majority are indifferent, though on the whole rather averse to it, while a few positively will not try at all.

A WATER JUMP.

The first thing to be done is to get your horse to take low and easy leaps without repugnance. For this purpose lay the bar you intend to use on the ground, and lead him over it without looking back at him or giving him any reason to suppose that you have any particular object in so doing. Should he object to stepping over it, be patient though firm, and when he has finally done so, pat and praise him; but if he has been bred in this country, and is used to bar places, he will probably give no trouble at this stage of his education. Now mount him and repeat the operation; then, having the bar raised a few inches, do so again, and continue doing so, always at a walk, until it is so high that he can no longer step over it. American horses are famous for their excellent tempers; nevertheless, at this point, unless you manage with care and with a judicious reference to equine peculiarities of mind and temper, you may meet with a refusal to proceed. In this event you must not use force or severity, or you may disgust the horse, perhaps forever, with the very exercise you wish him to learn to enjoy, but must content yourself with preventing him from sheering off and keeping him facing his task till, sooner or later, he will go over. Now praise him and make much of him, and ask no more jumping till the next lesson. It is not a good plan to put the bar up in an open place, for the horse will think it nonsense, and unless he is unusually docile will resent what will seem to him to be an imposition in forcing him to jump over it when he could easily go around it. A bar place or gate-way is much better, as it cannot be "flanked," and he will not wonder at being asked to go through it, but he should never be ridden backward and forward over the bar, nor allowed to see it raised, but should be brought around to it by a circuit which, if possible, should be large enough to make him forget the leaping, or think of it only as an accidental episode in the ride. The ground also should be no harder than good firm turf. Let him jump towards his stable or towards home by preference, and it will be well to let your assistant hold some little article of food which he is especially fond of in view just beyond the bar, so that his attention may be distracted from the effort, while an agreeable association is given him with it, and he is prevented from thinking that the obstacle is one of your making. Bear in mind that your object at present is threefold: to induce him to take a liking for the new exercise; to give him ease and confidence in the performance of it; and to train and strengthen by use the muscles brought into play, so that none of the unpleasant results mentioned above may follow. Therefore do not for a considerable time set the bar more than two feet high, but practise him at it several times a day; first, as already said, at a walk, then at a slow trot, and then at a canter, making him lead first with one foot, then with the other, until he not only springs over without touching and without apparently thinking anything about it, but shows by his lengthening or shortening his stride on approaching, so as to "take off" at the right distance, that his eye is becoming educated; and, finally, until a careful daily inspection of his feet and legs has proved that no soreness or tenderness anywhere is caused by this exercise. If he does not jump clean, but knocks the bar with his feet, it may be because he underestimates the height, as not only horses but men too are apt to do in the case of open fences made with posts and rails; therefore have a broad piece of board, two feet long, stood up against the bar like a post, and make him leap over it. If he still strikes, it will be well to try the plan which M. Baucher so enthusiastically recommends for all horses, and which consists in raising the bar a little just as the horse is in the act of springing.

It will be interesting to hear exactly what so great an authority has to say on this subject. After remarking that the bar should not be covered with anything to diminish its hardness, he proceeds: "I let two men hold the bare bar at six inches above the ground. The rider advances towards it at a walk, and at the moment when the horse, aided by the rider, takes the leap, the two men *raise the bar six inches.*" The horse naturally strikes his feet against it. "I make him begin again, until he clears the bar without touching, notwithstanding the repeated raising of it at each leap. Then I have the bar held at a foot above the ground, and, as before, it will be raised six inches at the moment of the leap. When the horse is accustomed to clear this new elevation, I have the bar gradually held six inches higher, still continuing to raise it six inches at each leap, and I thus succeed, after a few lessons given with the regular progression above described, in making all horses jump obstacles of a height that they would otherwise never have been able to clear. This simple proceeding, well applied, will be useful even to exceptional horses, such as steeple-chasers, by teaching them to come more carefully to the point of 'taking off,' and will render falls less frequent." The idea of M. Baucher is to get the horse in the habit of jumping a little higher than he thinks necessary, so as to be on the safe side, and a very good idea it is. It is a practice among experienced riders to hounds in England, instead of leaping a post-and-rail fence midway between the posts, to leap as close to a post as possible, or directly over it when it is not much higher than the rail.

To return to our equine scholar having practised him for a month or so at an elevation of two feet, his muscles will have adapted themselves to the new strain put upon them, and it will be safe to begin to raise the bar higher, and gradually to go up nearly to the limit of his ability. It is well, however, never to ask too much, as even a willing leaper will be sometimes so disgusted at what he thinks tyrannical exactions as to refuse obstinately ever to try again. The horse should never be allowed to rush at the bar, but should always, if approaching at a gallop, be collected, as much as a hundred feet away, so as to be under perfect control. The higher the leap, the slower the pace at which it should be taken, for the very momentum acquired by a rush, which would be useful in a water leap, would carry the animal against the bar instead of over it. The reins should be held in both hands, and after the horse has been collected with the curb, as may very likely be necessary, the curb should be relaxed, so that on approaching the leap he may feel only the gentle pressure of the snaffle, which will not make him fear to thrust forward his head, a fear which would possibly result in bringing him down on all fours at once, or even with the hind-feet first. As he rises to his leap, keep a steady but very gentle tension on the reins, being ready to support him firmly as his fore-feet touch the earth.

It is now time to experiment with low stone walls and with brooks, being always on your guard against those concealed man-traps in the shape of loose stones, which form one of the chief dangers of leaping in this country.

All this while we have been assuming the rider to be an accomplished horsewoman, and quite *au fait* at her fences. If, however, the business is entirely new to her, let her not be at all disheartened, for her own education can be carried on simultaneously with that of the horse, and without the least detriment to it. In this case, keep to the standing leap—that is, the leap taken from a walk—although it is really the most difficult to sit, until you can support the unusual motion without being in the least loosened in the saddle, and do not try the higher ones till you are perfect in the lower. The hands should be held as low as possible above the right

RISING TO THE LEAP.

knee, and pretty close to the body, so that they may have room to yield, and that the sudden thrusting out of the horse's head may not jerk you forward in the saddle, in which case the powerful impulsion of the hind-legs might pitch you out altogether. The advice is often given in books to lean forward and then backward in the leap, but the fact is that beginners, if they lean forward intentionally, seldom get back in time to avoid the shock above alluded to, and teachers, therefore, as well as friendly *coaches*, often call out "lean back" as a lady nears the bar, which results in giving the learner an awkward though perhaps not unsafe manner. The fact is that there is no necessity to try to lean forward, as the rising of the horse will bring you involuntarily into a position perpendicular to the ground, while the play of thigh and waist to prevent being tossed up is of the same kind as that in the gallop, only proportionately increased, and it will become instinctive if leaping is begun moderately and carried on progressively as already recommended. In coming down you can hardly lean too far back. The left foot should not be thrust forward, but kept straight, or drawn a very little back and held close against the horse's side; the stirrup, into which the foot is pushed to the instep, being one or two holes shorter than for ordinary riding. On approaching the fence, be particular to do nothing to distract the animal's attention, as, for instance, by ejaculations or nervous movements of

COMING DOWN.

the reins and person; and after the leap do not fail to reward him by praises and caresses, for it cannot be too deeply impressed on the mind that he is exceedingly sensitive to them, and will consider them an ample reward for his exertion.

The object of these instructions being to enable a lady to master the art of leaping without a regular instructor, it will not be amiss to sum up the advice already given at length, in the words of two competent authorities, "Vieille Moustache" and Mr. Sidney. The former says:

"She should take a firm hold of the upper crutch of the saddle with the right knee, sit well into the saddle—not back of it, because the farther back the greater the concussion when the horse alights—put her left foot well home in the stirrup, and press her left thigh firmly against the third crutch, while keeping the left knee flexible; lean slightly forward, avoid stiffening her waist, in order to throw the upper part of her figure backward at the right moment to preserve her balance. The hands must not move except with the body, and above all no attempt to enliven the horse by jagging his mouth as he is about to rise—a pernicious habit, practised by riders of both sexes who ought to know better. Reins too short, head too forward, and pace too violent are the ordinary faults of beginners. Women have on their saddles a firmer seat for leaping than men."

Mr. Sidney remarks: "A sheep hurdle is quite high

enough and the trunk of a tree is quite wide enough for the first steps in leaping. Balance, gripe of the pommels, and support of the stirrup must be combined; the seat as near the centre of the horse's back as the pommels will permit; the figure erect, not rigid, with the shoulders back, ready to bend gently backward as the horse rises in the air—not leaning forward, twisted over on the near side, like a popular spirited and absurd picture ("First at the Fence"), which really shows 'how not to do it;' the snaffle-reins held in both hands, at a length that will enable the horse fully to extend himself, and the rider to bear on his mouth as she bends back over his croup when he is landing. All this time her eyes should be looking between the horse's ears, so as to keep perfectly square in the saddle."

If the reader carries out the instruction already given with care, and exercises good sense and judgment, it is very unlikely that she will have a fall. Should this happen, however, there are two things to be remembered, first to get instantly away from the horse by scrambling or rolling, and secondly to keep hold of the reins. In any event, the timid may be reassured by reflecting that a fall is usually without any serious result, it being by no means as dangerous to come down with the horse as to be thrown from him.

PART IV.
BUYING A SADDLE-HORSE.

The opening of the horse-market is not announced to ladies by cards of invitation, though such an innovation on the old-fashioned methods might prove a great success in the hands of a skilful dealer. Nevertheless, as soon as spring opens, all over the United States, ladies are " shopping " for horses, but by no means in their usual jaunty and self-confident way, for their eyes, which do them such good service at the silk or lace counter, take on a timid and hesitating expression in the presence of this unwonted problem. The acquisition of a saddle-horse by a young girl is usually a long and complicated operation, in the course of which her hopes are alternately raised and depressed day by day, to be at last very likely disappointed altogether. It often begins at breakfast-time, somewhat in the following fashion : " Dear papa, don't you think I might have a saddle-horse this season ? Eleanor B——'s uncle has given her a beauty, and we could ride together; and you know that is just the sort of exercise the doctor said would be good for me." The father hesitates, and few fathers there are who do not in their hearts long to grant the request; but he is a very busy man, and does not feel as if he could take any more cares upon his shoulders; and very likely he knows little about horses, and really has not the slightest idea how to set about such a purchase; and his mind misgives him as he remembers what he has heard of the tricks of dealers. So he says, "Oh, my dear, I don't see how we can manage it. We should be cheated, to begin with, and pay twice as much as he is worth, and he would run away and throw you off; and then he would be always sick, and finally fall lame, and would have to be given away before the season is over." This is the critical point of this part of the little family transaction, and if the daughter has nothing more convincing to offer in reply than some vague statement that she is sure she sees plenty of good horses in the street, and that she does not see why her horse should be sick any more than any one else's, and that there must be plenty of good men to take care of him to be had at low wages, then probably her case is lost. But suppose that she replies: "Oh yes, papa, I *know* a horse that will do *nicely* and can't be sickly for he has worked all summer and not lost *a day* and he is eight years old and so has eaten all his wild oats by this time and he isn't a very pretty color but then we can buy him cheaper for that reason and I don't care so much for color as I do for *shape* and he is *very* well formed indeed his legs and feet are excellent and he has a broad shoulder and a pretty neck and head and we gave him a long drive the other day and he never missed *a step* and he isn't afraid of anything and I drove him fast up a steep hill and jumped out at the top to give him a bunch of clover and took the opportunity to listen to his breathing and to feel his pulse and there is nothing the matter with *his* heart or wind I assure you and I will promise to go to the stable once a day to see him." Then the chances are that, after laughing at the long sentence without a stop, and telling her she is a runaway filly herself, papa will say, " Well, suppose we take a look at this wonderful animal; we are not obliged to buy him, you know, unless we please, and I don't say what I may decide finally," and her case is won. To be able, however, to make the reply above supposed, simple as it sounds, indicates a very unusual amount of observation for a young girl.

There are many ladies who can at a glance tell real point lace from artificial, be the imitation never so good; but there are comparatively few who know the points of a horse, or can detect any but the most glaring defects or blemishes. The reason is simply want of practice, for the difference between the well-made and the ill-made horse, or between the sound animal and the spavined or foundered one, is far greater than that between the two pieces of lace above mentioned, which to most masculine eyes would appear exactly alike. With her superior delicacy of observation and quickness of perception, a woman ought to be, other things supposed equal, a better judge of horses than a man, and there must surely be a great many who, if they really believed this, would think it worth their while to master the small vocabulary of technical terms in which the information they require is always couched, and such would speedily find their reward in the opening of a new and interesting field of research. To begin with, how few ladies so much as know the names of the different parts of the animal! Head, legs, and body, eyes, ears, and tail, are about all the words in the feminine dictionary of horse lore, and whether the pasterns are not a disease of colts, the coronet a part of a bridle, and the frog a swelling in the throat, my lady knoweth not. A half-hour, however, given to the illustration on the following page, will remove once for all this preliminary difficulty, and will open the way to a consideration of the proper form and motion of the parts of which the names are here given:

PARTS AND "POINTS" OF THE HORSE, ALPHABETICALLY ARRANGED.

Arm, or True Arm (8, 8).—Extends from the point of the shoulder (29) to the elbow (10). It should be long.

Back.—This is one of the four parts which, according to Arab saying, should be short.

Back Sinew.—The powerful muscle back of the cannon-bone. It should be free from contact with the bone.

Barrel, or Chest.—Should be roomy, as not only the lungs, but all the organs of digestion, are contained in it.

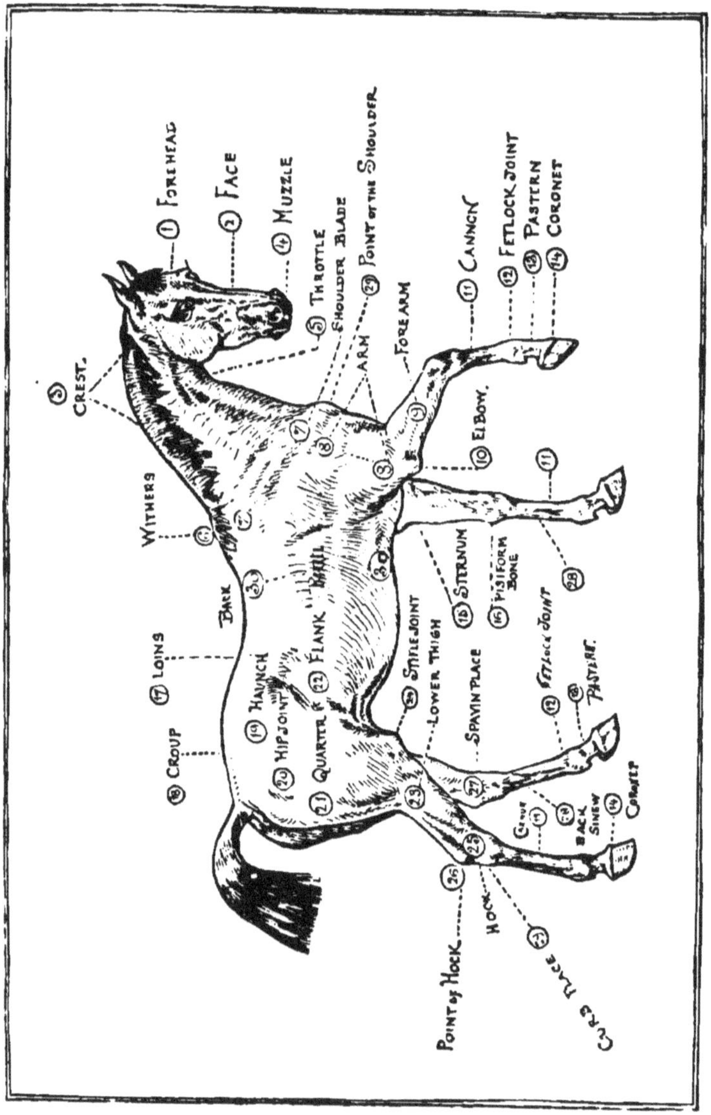

136 HORSEMANSHIP FOR WOMEN.

Belly.—This is one of the four parts which the Arab proverb says must be long.

Breast, or Bosom.—Should be deep, but not too broad, or speed will be diminished.

Cannon-bone (11).—The strong oval bone stretching between the knee and fetlock-joint in the fore-leg, and between the hock and fetlock-joint in the hind-leg.

Chin Groove.—The place just above the swell of the lower lip, in which the curb-chain should lie.

Coronet (14).—A cartilaginous band encircling the top of the hoof.

Crest.—The upper part of the back of the neck.

Croup (18).—Strictly speaking, the upper part of hind-quarters between hip and tail, but in a general way taken for that part of the body back of the saddle.

Curb-place (29).—A part of the hind-leg, six or eight inches below the point of the hock, where "curbs," or enlargement of the back sinew resulting from strain, are to be looked for.

Ear.—Neither too long nor very short.

Elbow (10).—Should not be nearly under the point of the shoulder, but considerably back of it, and should neither be turned out nor pressed against the ribs.

Eye.—Should be clear and full, and of a gentle expression.

Fetlock.—The tuft of hair at the back of the pastern-joint. When thick and coarse it indicates common blood.

Fetlock-joint (12).—Is between the shank and the pastern, and is the same as pastern-joint.

Flank (22).

Forearm (9).—Should be long and muscular.

Forehead.—The broader, the more sense and courage. The average of six thorough-bred English horses was nine and a half inches.

Frog.—The triangular piece in centre of bottom of hoof.

Gaskin, or Lower Thigh (23).—Should be strong and long, reaching well down. Measured from the stifle-joint to the point of hock should be twenty-eight inches in a well-bred horse of fifteen hands and three-quarters.

Girth (30, 30).—Gives approximately the capacity of the lungs.

Heel.—Should not be too high or contracted, that is, drawn together.

Hip.—Should be broad, with powerful muscles.

Hip-joint (20).—Is not always easily discovered by an amateur.

Hock (25).—One of the most important of the points of the horse; should be large, clean—that is, without any rough protuberances on the bone—flat, and "with a good clean point standing clear of the rest of the joint."

Hoof.—Deep, like a cup; not flat, like a saucer.

Jaw.—Should be wide up toward the socket, to give room for windpipe, and permit of a graceful carriage of head.

Knee.—Can hardly be too large. Looked at from in front, should appear much wider than the leg, and should stretch out backward into a sharp edge, called the pisiform-bone.

Loins (17).—Broad, muscular, and arched slightly upward.

Lower Thigh.—See "Gaskin" (23).

Mane.—When thick and coarse, indicates inferior blood.

Muzzle (4).—Should be small, but with large nostril. A coarse muzzle indicates low breeding.

Nostril.—Open and prominent.

Pastern (13).—The short oblique bone between the fetlock and hoof. Should not be straighter than sixty, nor lower than forty-five degrees to the ground.

Pastern-joint (12).—Same as fetlock-joint.

Pisiform-bone (16).—At the back of the knee.

Point of the Hock (26).

Point of the Shoulder (29).—The lower end of the shoulder-blade, to which is jointed the true arm.

Poll.—The top of the head.

Quarters (21).—Should be muscular.

Ribs.—Should be well arched, and come up close to the hip.

Shoulder (7, 7).—Should be long and oblique.

Spavin Place (27).—Should be free from bony enlargement.

Stifle-joint (24).—Corresponds to the human knee.

Tail.—Not set on too high, but yet carried gracefully.

Thigh, or True Thigh.—Reaches from hip-joint to stifle. Should be long to give speed.

Thrapple, or Throttle (5).—Upper part of throat.

True Arm (8, 8).—See "Arm." To a careless observer it appears to form part of the shoulder.

Withers (6).—It is the height of the withers which gives the height of the horse.

To be a "good judge of a horse" is indeed an accomplishment as rare as it is desirable; but while it cannot be taught by word of mouth or pen, yet a few principles may be acquired which will be of great assistance in cultivating the eye. Even if the judgment be never so thoroughly formed as to be a safe guide unaided in purchasing, yet a great deal of pleasure may be derived from noting the comparative excellences of the really fine horses constantly to be seen in this country; and there is no reason in the world why a lady's opinion on this subject should continue to weigh as little as it has generally done hitherto. A graceful neck and an air of spirit usually win the feminine suffrages, yet often co-exist with a long back, spindle-shanks, and a chest both shallow and narrow. Nevertheless, a good neck is an excellent thing, and so is a small head, especially if it have a wide forehead; but next look to see if there is also (to use a horsey expression), "a short back and a long belly," a deep chest, a sloping shoulder, and legs broad and long above the knee and hock, but broad and short below.

The Arabs have a proverb that "there should be four points of a horse long, four short, and four broad." The long are the neck, the forearm, the thigh, and the belly; the short are the back, the pastern, the tail, and the ear; the broad are the forehead, the chest, the croup, and the limbs. The head should be small and bony; that of an English thorough-bred of fifteen and three-quarter hands will measure twenty-two to twenty-four inches in length, with the forehead eight to ten inches broad, the face dishing below the eyes. The withers should be high, the shoulder as broad as possible—not fleshy, but bony—and lying at an angle of about forty-five degrees. The chest should be broad and deep, to give room for lungs and heart. The knees should be broad, the hoofs large, and not flat, but deep.

The reasons for some of the above recommendations may be made clearer by a rough comparison between the frame of the horse and that of man. For instance, the shoulder of the former, from the withers to its forward point at the joint, is equivalent to the shoulder-blade and collar-bone of the latter, and a broad shoulder is as sure an indication of strength in the one as in the other. If the horse is "short above and long below," it gives him a carriage similar to that of a man with a full, broad chest, who holds his head high and his shoulders back.

The knee of the horse corresponds to the human wrist, and his *hock*, or "back knee," as the children call it, to our heel. The shank of the fore-leg, then, or the part between the knee and fetlock, corresponds to the hand, and the hoof and pastern to the fingers; while the shank of the hind-leg, or the part between hock and fetlock, corresponds to our foot, the hoof and pastern being the toes. The horse may thus be said to walk upon the tips of his fingers and toes, and it will readily be seen why the leg weakens in proportion as the pastern and shank lengthen. The arm proper of the horse is very short and almost concealed from view, reaching from the forward point of the shoulder to the elbow, which is close against the side.

The more oblique the shoulder, the greater the power of this arm to throw the forearm forward, so as to support the body in the gallop, and in coming down from a leap. A straight shoulder is adapted for pulling loads, but is not fit for the saddle, except upon level roads, becoming positively dangerous in broken ground. The two upper members of the hind-leg, reaching from the hip to the hock, are together commonly called the thigh, as the thigh proper, which stretches from the hip to the stifle-joint, is very short and almost concealed from observation. The stifle-joint, which corresponds to our knee, lies close against the flank. Read the description, to some extent traditional, of the wonderful mare Swallow, in Kingsley's "Hereward the Wake." She was evidently not from Arab stock, with her big ugly head; but horses — like men and women — of extraordinary strength, and beauty too, are sometimes happened upon in the most unlikely places. Indeed, in many an ungraceful form there is stored up an amount of vital energy which explains the saying that one can find " good horses of all shapes." Nevertheless, the presumption is always in favor of the well-shaped animal, and the acknowledged type of equine beauty is the English thorough-bred. This is of pure Arab blood, but so improved by many generations of careful breeding and training that it now excels not only all other European and Oriental races but the modern Arab himself, that is considered to be, weight for weight, twenty - five per cent. stronger than other breeds. One invariable mark of Arab blood, by-the-bye, is a high and graceful carriage of the tail. The eye should be kind and quiet, that of an Arab very gentle, even sleepy, when at rest, but full of fire and animation when in motion.

" The relative proportions of and exact shape desirable in each of the points described varies considerably in the several breeds. Thus, when speed and activity are essential, an oblique shoulder-blade is a *sine quâ non*, while for heavy harness it can hardly be too upright. *There are some elements, however, which are wanted in any horse, such as big hocks and knees, flat legs with large sinews, open jaws* (that is, with the lower jaw-bones wide apart), *and full nostrils.*"

It is well, after taking a general look at a horse and getting an impression of him as a whole, to divide him up mentally into sections, and examine these in detail one after the other. Taking first the head, which should be bony, not fleshy, remember that the more brain the more "horse sense." Next look at the neck, which should be neither too thick nor too long, but connecting head and shoulders by a graceful sweep. Then the forequarters, observing that the shoulder-blade and true arm are both long, well supplied though not loaded with muscle, and join each other at the point of the shoulder at a rather sharp angle. Then the "middle-piece," which should be rounded in the barrel, arched slightly in the loin, "short above and long below," and well ribbed up towards the hip. Next the hind-quarters, then the legs, knees, hocks, and feet, observing that the knees are firm, the cannon-bones and pastern are flat and strong, and that the back sinew is strong and stands free from the bone.

Now have the horse set in motion, and observe him first from one side, then from the other, and then from behind, noting the carriage and movements of the different parts in the order above given. This examination is practically the more important of the two.

Let no one suppose that mere verbal instruction, however judicious and elaborate, will, without practice, make a good judge of horse-flesh any more than it will of Brussels point-lace. All it is here intended to do is to aid in training the eye, which must be constantly exercised upon whatever specimens may come before it, comparing them mentally with one another, and noting their defects and qualities whether of form or of motion. It will soon be found that such observations, particularly when relating to the motions of the horse, have a fascination peculiarly their own, and open a new and wide field of amusement.

In examining a horse a lady cannot of course usually make the thorough inspection personally which would be necessary to warrant his limbs and wind perfectly sound, but she can, by taking a little time to it, form an opinion which will be very nearly correct. She should first master the vocabulary at the end of this chapter, which will give her an idea what defects to be on the lookout for, and just where to seek for them; and she should cultivate her eye at every opportunity by scanning critically every horse she sees—or, to be more moderate, say one or two a day—endeavoring to detect a "spavin" or "curb," or what not, which the owner does not suspect or perhaps shuts his eyes to. Then, when a horse is brought up for her approval, let her take her own time, refuse to be hurried or humbugged, but, as already suggested, look him over from all sides, at rest and in motion, and finally *get him on trial for a week*. This last precaution is the most valuable of all, and worth, as "Stonehenge" says, ten per cent. on the price of the animal, and it can very often be obtained by the simple offer of paying for his services in case he is not purchased; indeed, some of the most successful New York City dealers grant this privilege to any responsible customer as a matter of course. To return to our inspection: First take a side view from a little distance, observing that he stands perpendicularly on all four legs, bearing equal weight on each; any "pointing," or putting forward of a forefoot to relieve it of its share of weight, being indicative of tenderness if not lameness. Notice the size, shape, and relative proportion of the different parts, and scrutinize them carefully for swellings, or for weakened or deformed joints. Then do the same from before, then from behind. Now have him led past you, first at a walk, then at a slow trot, insisting that the groom shall not take him by the headstall, but by the end of the halter, so as to leave him free to nod his head if he pleases. Now have him saddled and bridled, and all his paces shown, finishing with a smart gallop long enough to sweat him well, after which listen carefully to his breathing, which should be noiseless; observe that the heaving of the flanks is regular and not spasmodic, and that the beating of the heart is not violent or irregular. During your week of trial take some disinterested person with you to serve as witness in case of accident or misconduct, and work the horse hard every day, so as to be sure that he does not lose his appetite when fatigued, but being careful not to injure his feet by galloping on hard roads, or to let him slip or strain himself in any way. Remember the oft-quoted words of the English stable-man: "It ain't the speed that 'urts the 'orse; it's the 'ammer, 'ammer, 'ammer on the 'ard 'igh-road." After your first ride, leave the saddle on for twenty minutes with the girths slackened,

THE SORT OF HORSE TO BUY.

and next morning, before putting it on again, examine the back carefully for any soreness or puffy spot, and if such exist, abstain from riding until it has quite disappeared, for a day of patience now is better than a week after a saddle-gall has become fairly established. The saddle, of course, should fit the horse well, and there should always be a free space along above the backbone and withers.

The cut on the preceding page shows a saddle-horse of the very best form for a lady's use.

The color of a horse is an important factor in the price, except in the case of animals of extraordinary qualities; and although different persons have their special preferences, yet probably the order of the following list will give the average taste of the horse-buying public:

1. Blood bay with black points; that is, with mane, tail, and legs from the knee downward black.
2. Rich chestnut.
3. Rich brown.
4. Common bay with black points.
5. Common chestnut.
6. Dark dapple gray.
7. Full black.
8. Light bay with brown legs.
9. White.
10. Common gray.
11. Brownish-black.
12. Sorrel.

When your decision is finally made, obtain (from the person selling) a warranty, which had better be written upon the bill itself, giving the height, age, and color of the horse, and stating that he is sound, kind, goes well under the saddle and in single or double harness, and is afraid of nothing.

The vices which in the eye of the law make a horse returnable are Biting, Cribbing, Kicking, Rearing when dangerous, and Shying when dangerous.

In estimating the height of a horse it is convenient to remember that fifteen hands make exactly five feet —a "hand" being four inches, or a third of a foot.

To aid the inexperienced we give a cut showing a horse, originally of high spirit but faulty organization, broken down by ill usage, and also append a list of the various defects and ailments which every horse-owner ought to know something about.

LIST OF DISEASES AND DEFECTS.

[Those printed in small capitals constitute UNSOUNDNESS in the eye of the law.]

Acclimation.—Horses removed from one part of the country to another have usually a period of indisposition, often of severe illness, and always for some time require more than ordinary care. It is well, therefore, not to buy a Western horse in the Atlantic States until he has been at least a month in his new surroundings.

Apoplexy.—Sometimes called "sleepy staggers." Begins with drowsiness, passing into insensibility, with snoring respiration, and ending in death.

BLINDNESS.—Often comes on gradually. Eyes of a bluish-black are thought suspicious, as is inflammation of ball or lid, or cloudiness of pupil.

BLIND STAGGERS.—See "Megrims" and "Staggers."

BOG-SPAVIN.—A soft swelling on the inner side of the hock-joint towards the front. It is caused by the formation of a sac contain-

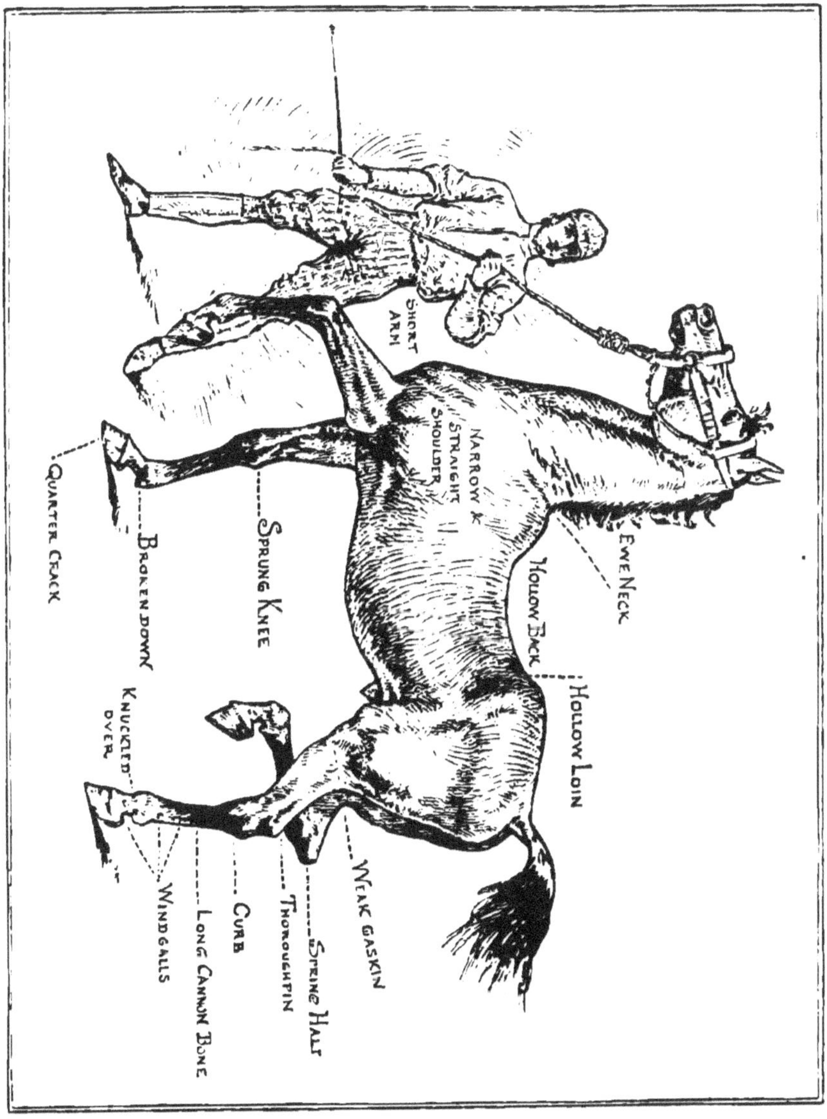

BUYING A SADDLE-HORSE. 149

THE SORT OF HORSE NOT TO BUY.

ing synovial fluid which has oozed out of the joint. The result usually of brutality. Incurable.

BLOOD-SPAVIN.—A swelling in nearly the same place caused by an aneurism or sac of arterial blood. Incurable. Very rare.

BONE-SPAVIN.—A swelling caused by a bony growth on the inside of the hock-joint towards the front. It produces lameness, which sometimes passes off temporarily after a few minutes' work. Sometimes curable. This is what is usually meant by spavin.

Bots.—Caused by the larvæ of the bot-fly, which cling to the lining of the stomach by their two hooks till after several months they reach maturity and pass out with the droppings. They seem to do little harm, and should be left alone, as they cannot be destroyed by any medicine safe for a horse to take.

BREAKING DOWN.—A rupture of the tendons of the leg causing the fetlock-joint to give way downward. Incurable.

Broken Knee.—Indicated by white or bare spots, showing that the horse has been down, and is presumably a stumbler.

BROKEN WIND.—Accompanied by a husky cough, and indicated by heaving flanks and forcible double respiration after exercise. Incurable.

Capped Hock.—A soft movable swelling on point of hock, caused by a bruise, usually got in kicking.

CATARACT.—Opacity of the crystalline lens of the eye.

Chapped Heels.—Always the result of neglect. Often accompanied by fever and constitutional disturbance.

Cold.—Shown by dulness, rough coat, loss of appetite, tears and running at the nose. Give soft food and nurse well without exercise.

Colic.—Distinguished from inflammation of the bowels by intervals of quiet between the spasms, and by the fact that the horse will strike his belly violently in the hope of relief. Give first a warm injection, to remove any obstruction in lower bowel, and then administer stimulants.

Contracted Heels.—Often caused by improper shoeing, but often natural, and in this case producing no ill result.

CORNS.—Do not at all resemble human corns. A corn is a reddish and very sensitive spot in the sole of the foot under the shoe, caused by a rupture of the delicate blood-vessels, resulting in an abnormal fungoid growth.

Costiveness.—May bring on "blind staggers" in a horse inclined to this disease. No horse should be hurried when first taken out till his bowels have been moved.

COUGH.—Constitutes unsoundness while it lasts. Caused by foul air, dusty food, irregular work. Crush the oats, damp the hay, and give linseed tea for drink.

CRIBBING, *or* CRIB-BITING.—Is sometimes considered a vice, but is doubtless a result of indigestion. The horse lays hold of the manger with his teeth, straightens his neck, sucks wind into his stomach, and ejects gas. Probably some alkali, say lime-water or baking soda, would be beneficial.

CURB.—A soft, painful swelling on the back of the hind-leg six or eight inches below the hock. See illustration.

Cutting.—See "Interfering" and "Speedy Cut."

Discharge from Nostril.—Is usually caused by a simple cold, but may be a symptom of the contagious and incurable disease GLANDERS, and proximity to it should therefore be carefully avoided.

Distemper.—A disease of young horses, occurring once only. See "Strangles."

Ewe Neck.—Carries the head high and nearly in a horizontal position, so that the bit has not a proper bearing on the "bars," but is inclined to slip back towards the grinders.

FARCY.—An incurable and contagious disease, caused by blood-poisoning, and indicated by sores usually on inside of thigh, or on neck and hips. As it is communicable to human beings, every farcied horse should be immediately killed. It is well to avoid all approach to horses having sores of any kind. See "Glanders."

Filled Legs.—A swelled condition of the lower parts, usually caused by want of exercise, and relieved by bandaging and rubbing.

Fistula of the Withers.—An abscess among the muscles over the shoulder-blades, usually caused by pressure of saddle upon the bony ridge of back. Requires surgical operation.

Forging.—See "Overreaching."

FOUNDER, OR FEVER IN THE FEET.—An inflammation of the parts between the crust of the foot and the pedal-bone, including the *laminæ*, which cease to secrete horn. It is caused sometimes by hard roads, and sometimes by eating or drinking or standing in a draught of air when heated. This name is commonly applied to any rheumatic lameness of the fore-feet or legs brought on as above, whether its seat be the feet, the tendons of the legs, or the muscles of the breast, in which last case it is called "chest-founder." The treatment, which is only palliative, is hot bathing and friction with liniments.

Gadfly Bites.—Often very annoying. May be prevented by washing legs and flanks with a strong tea of green elder bark.

Galls—from saddle.—Best prevented by leaving the saddle in place for twenty minutes after loosening the girths. When occurring, however, should receive prompt attention, as they are very tedious if neglected. Examine the back carefully after the first ride on a new horse, and also before putting on the saddle the next day.

GLANDERS.—A disgusting, contagious, and incurable disease, the chief symptom of which is a discharge from one nostril, at first transparent, then slightly sticky, then thick and yellow. As it is highly contagious to human beings, in whom it is equally dreadful and always fatal, *a glandered horse should be instantly killed, as the law requires.* It is well to avoid all horses having any discharge, however slight, from the nose. Glanders may be caught from "farcy," and *vice versa.*

GRAPES.—A filthy and incurable disease of heels and pastern, caused by gross neglect. It is the last stage of "grease."

GREASE.—An aggravated form of "chapped heels," accompanied by swelling, fever and a serous discharge. Wash clean frequently, and anoint with Dalley's salve.

Gripes.—See "Colic."

HEART DISEASE.—May be detected by auscultation. Incurable. Ends in sudden death.

HEAVES.—See "Broken Wind."

Hide-bound.—The skin appears too tight, and as if fast to the ribs. It is caused by a disordered stomach, and requires nourishing food.

Inflammation of Bowels.—The pain is continuous, and the horse is careful not actually to strike his belly with his feet. Requires, of course, very different treatment from colic, but an injection should be the first thing done.

Interfering.—Striking the fetlock-joint with the foot. Caused sometimes by weakness and fatigue, but usually by bad shoeing, and a good blacksmith is the best adviser.

Lampas.—A swelling of the gums, relieved by lancing

KNEE-SPRUNG.—Incurable. Result of overwork.

KNUCKLED.—Same as "set over." A condition of the fetlock-joint corresponding to that of the "sprung" knee.

LAMINITIS.—The scientific name of "founder."

MAD STAGGERS.—Violent insanity, caused by inflammation of the brain. The last stage sometimes of sleepy staggers. Incurable.

Mallenders.—A scurvy patch at the back of the knee, caused by neglect, and not obstinate.

Mange.—An itch produced by a parasitic insect.

MEGRIMS.—A falling-sickness like epilepsy. It begins with a laying back of the ears and shaking of the head; is accompanied by convulsions; and passes off of itself in two or three minutes, the horse appearing to be none the worse. Often called "Blind Staggers."

NAVICULAR DISEASE.—An ulceration of the navicular-joint in the foot, causing lameness; incurable, except by extirpation of the nerve.

NERVED.—A nerved horse has had one of the nerves of the foot cut to remove the pain and lameness caused by the "navicular disease."

OPHTHALMIA.—A purulent inflammation of the eye. Epidemic.

ORGANIC DISEASE of the bony system anywhere constitutes unsoundness.

Overreaching.—Striking the toe of the front-foot with the toe of the hind-foot; sometimes called "clicking." Often remedied by shoeing.

Poll-evil.—An abscess in the top of the neck, near the head, caused by a blow.

PUMICE FOOT.—Bulging sole, weak crust, the result of "laminitis." Incurable.

Quarter Crack.—Occurs usually on the inside of fore-foot. A bad sign, as well as very slow and troublesome to cure.

QUIDDING.—Dropping the food half chewed from the mouth. Indicative of sore throat.

QUITTOR.—Burrowing abscess in the foot.

Rheumatism.—Cause, effect, and treatment the same as for human beings.

RING-BONE.—An enlargement of the bone by growth, a little above the coronet.

ROARING.—Caused by a contraction of windpipe. Incurable.

RUPTURES of all kinds constitute unsoundness.

Saddle-gall.—Swelling caused by chafing of saddle. If the skin is broken it is called a "sitfast;" if not, a "warble."

Sallenders.—Scurvy patch in front of hock-joint.

Sand Crack.—Occurs on the inside of fore-foot and on the toe of the hind-foot.

Scratches.—See "Chapped Heels."

Scouring.—Looseness of the bowels.

SEEDY TOE.—A separation of the crust of the hoof from the laminæ, the result of laminitis. Scarcely curable.

SIDE-BONE.—A bony growth just above the coronet, causing lameness. Incurable.

SPAVIN.—See "Bone, Blood, and Bog Spavin."

Speedy Cut.—A cut of the knee from the foot of opposite leg. Dangerous, because the pain often causes the horse to fall.

STAGGERS.—See "Apoplexy." "Sleepy," "Trotting," and "Mad" Staggers are different forms and stages of the same disease, caused usually by overfeeding.

Strangles, or Colt Distemper.—A severe swelling of the glands of the throat, which gathers and breaks.

STRING-HALT *or* SPRING-HALT.—A peculiar snatching up of the hind-leg, caused by some nervous disorder. Incurable.

Surfeit. — An eruption of round, blunt spots, caused by heating food.

THICK WIND. — Defective respiration without noise. Incurable.

THICKENING OF BACK SINEWS. — Result of strain.

THRUSH. — An offensive discharge from the frog, the result of inflammation, caused by want of cleanliness or overwork, etc.

THOROUGH-PIN. — A sac of synovial fluid formed between the bones of the hock from side to side.

Warble. — A saddle-gall when simply swollen but not broken.

Warts. — Should be removed, as they tend to spread.

WHIRLBONE LAMENESS. — Lameness of hip-joint.

Windgalls, or *Puffs.* — Little oval swellings just above the fetlock-joint between the back sinew and the bone.

Worms. — Sometimes troublesome, but less so than often supposed.

WHISTLING. — Caused by a contraction of windpipe. Incurable.

INDEX.

ACCLIMATION, 148.
Advancing at Touch of Heel, 41, 44.
Amateur Horse-training, 1.
Amble, 28.
Apoplexy, 148.
Appel, 28.
Approaching a Fence, 119.
Arm, 135.
Arrière-main, 23.
Avant-main, 28.

BACK, 135.
Back Sinew, 135
Backing, 75, 76.
Barrel, or Chest, 135.
Bars, 15.
Belly, 137.
Bending the Neck to Right and Left, 32, 35, 48, 49.
Biting, 148.
Blind Staggers, 148.
Blindness, 148.
Blood-spavin, 150.
Bone-spavin, 150.
Boring, 150.
Bots, 150.
Breaking Down, 150.

Breast, or Bosom, 137.
Bridles, 12.
Bridle-tooth, 15, 18.
Broken Knee, 150.
Buying a Saddle-horse, 132.

CANNON-BONE, 137.
Cantering, 64.
Capped Hock, 150.
Cataract, 150.
Cavesson, 46.
Changing the Leading Foot, 66, 79.
Chapped Heels, 150.
Chin Groove, 15, 29, 137.
Cold, 150.
Colic, 150.
Color, 147.
Contracted Heels, 150.
Corns, 150.
Coronet, 137.
Costiveness, 151.
Cough, 151.
Crest, 137.
Cribbing, 148, 151.
Croup, 38, 137.
Curb-place, 137.
Curbs, 151.
Cutting, 151.

DEUX PISTES, 29, 71.
Discharge from Nostrils, 12, 15.
Diseases and Defects, 148.
Distemper, 151.
Dress, 88.
Duke of Wellington, 110.
Dumb-jockey, 46.

EAR, 137.
Elbow, 29, 137.
Etiquette in the Saddle, 87.
Ewe Neck, 151.
Eye, 137.

"FALLING THROUGH," 16.
Farcy, 151.
Fetlock, 29, 137.
Filled Legs, 151.
Fistula of the Withers, 151.
Flank, 137.
Flexion of the Jaw, 32.
Flexions de la Mâchoire, 21.
Flexions de l'Encolure, 32.
Flying Trot, 58.
Fore-arm, 29, 137.
Forehand, 38.
Forehead, 137.
Forge, 29.
Forging, 152.
Founder, or Fever in the Feet, 152.
Frog, 29, 137.

GADFLY BITES, 152.
Galloping, 64.
Galls, 152.
Gaskin, or Lower Thigh, 137.
"Getting a Horse accustomed to Skirts," 42.
Girths, 138.

Glanders, 152.
Going on *Deux Pistes*, 72.
Grapes, 152.
Grease, 152.
Grinders, 29.
Gripes, 152.
Groom, 116.
Guiding Bridlewise, 55.

HAND, 29, 104.
Hand-gallop, 29, 64.
Heart Disease, 152.
Heaves, 153.
Heel, 138.
Hide-bound, 153.
Hip, 138.
Hock, 29, 138.
Holding the Bit lightly, 21, 24.
Hoof, 138.
Horse-training is not Horse-breaking, 9.

INTERFERING, 28, 153.

JAW, 138.
Jog-trot, 58.

KICKING, 69.
Knee, 138.
Knee-sprung, 153.
Knuckled, 153.

LAMINITIS, 153.
Lampas, 153.
Leading with Left Fore-foot, 88.
Leading with Right Fore-foot, 80.
Leaping, 118.
Loins, 138.
Lower Thigh, 138.

Lowering the Head, 25, 28.
Lunging-cord, 46.

MAD STAGGERS, 153.
Mallenders, 153.
Mane, 138.
Manége, 29.
Mange, 153.
Megrims, 153.
Method of holding Reins in both Hands, 111.
Méthode d'Équitation, Baucher, 4.
Mount, 91.
Mounting, 92.
Moving the Croup to Right and Left, 38, 52.
Muzzle, 138.

NAVICULAR DISEASE, 153.
Nerved, 153.
Nippers, 30.
Nostrils, 138.

ON THE ROAD, 107.
On which Side to Ride, 100.
"One, Two, Three," 95.
Ophthalmia, 153.
Ordinary Pirouette, 71.
Organic Disease, 153.
Overreaching, 153.

PACE, 30.
Pacing, 192.
Parts and Points of a Horse, 138.
Passage, 30, 71, 73, 138.
Pastern, 30.
Pastern-joint, 138.
Piaffer, 30.
Pirouettes, 30, 71.

Pisiform-bone, 138.
Piste, 30, 74.
Placing the Foot in the Stirrup, 96.
Poll, 30, 138.
Poll-evil, 154.
Position in Saddle, 97.
"Pulling the Hands steadily Apart," 33.
Pulling the Right Rein, 36.
Pumice Foot, 154.
Punishment in Case of Resistance, 27.

QUARTER CRACK, 154.
Quarters, 138.
Quidding, 154.
Quittor, 154.

RACK, 30.
Ramener, 30.
Rassembler, 30.
Ready to Mount, 94.
Rearing, 66, 148.
Reins, Act of Changing, 77.
Reins in Hand, 43, 77.
Rheumatism, 154.
Riding in Circles, 79.
Ring-bone, 154.
Rising to the Leap, 127.
Roaring, 154.
Running Away, 69.
Ruptures, 154.

SADDLE-GALL, 154.
Saddles, 12, 13.
Sand Crack, 154.
Scouring, 154.
Scratches, 154.
Seat, 102, 103.

INDEX.

Seedy Toe, 154.
Shank, 30.
Shoulder, 138.
Shying, 68.
Side-bone, 154.
Sidney, Mr., 130.
Single-foot, 30.
Snaffle, 30.
Spavins and Splints, 30, 138, 154.
Speedy Cut, 154.
Staggers, 154.
Starting, 99.
Stifle-joint, 31, 138.
Stopping at Touch of Whip on Back, 45.
Strangles, 154.
String-halt, 154.
Style, 50.
Surcingle, 31.
Surfeit, 155.

TAIL, 134.
Thick Wind, 155.

Thickening of Back Sinews, 155.
Thigh, 31, 139.
Thorough-pin, 155.
Thrapple, or Throttle, 139.
Throat-latches, 15, 31.
Thrush, 155.
Trotting, 58.
True Arm, 139.
Turning, 112.

VICES, 148.
" Vieille Moustache," 130.

WALKING, 46, 51.
Warble, 155.
Warts, 155.
Water Jump, 121.
Whips, 13.
Whirlbone Lameness, 155.
Whistling, 155.
Windgalls, 155.
Withers, 31, 139.
Worms, 155.

www.ingramcontent.com/pod-product-compliance
Lightning Source LLC
Chambersburg PA
CBHW022118160426
43197CB00009B/1071